myles j. swain

a Broken Cradle

Llumina
PRESS

ISBN: 978-1-62550-511-8

For Taron, my sun and moon

and everything in between—my daughter and greatest love.

For Lugnut—my little Lugnut,

always reach for your star . . . Go, Batman.

For Kevin, who found it within his heart

to fall in love with my greatest love.

To everyone else, my wish is that, in reading my story, you will

find a small part to connect with or relate to. Upon doing so, we

will have become a part of one another.

Acknowledgments

Thanks, Stacey, for always giving me a soft place to land.

I would like to give special thanks to Julia and Dorothy, for all their support during the writing of this book. Your friendship has meant more than you'll ever know.

Thank you, Susan, for continually reminding me all those years that I needed to write a book about my life.

i feel the dark winds,

my name, written like sand,

embedded in the shadows of dreams,

calls out in the distance;

i am alone.

i have no boundary—

time has given no direction

to follow the echoes;

i have only a need

to find my name.

mjs

Introduction

I've just gotten home from spending the day with my family—my daughter, my son-in-law, and my grandson. My grandson is into Batman right now. And he knows all the characters that go with Batman. He has watched the DVD at least a hundred times. The Lugnut will be two years old in three months.

I thought being a father was the best that it got, but being Poppy to that little Lugnut is indescribable. He calls me Poppy 'cause my daughter calls me Papa. She has called me that her whole life. It was her first word.

Everything seems so normal—as it should be. Normalcy is something I welcome wholeheartedly, with open arms. It's been a long time coming, as it wasn't so long ago that my life was anything but normal.

Most of the events here I have never spoken about or shared with anyone, with the exception of my brother.

No matter where I am in this life, no matter where my mind is at the moment, I can't seem to let go of the clutter. Somewhere in those early stages, in the deepest part of my being, it grabbed hold of my core. It securely attached itself to the fragments—bound to the bits, the pieces, always trying to hide. It slid into the darkness of my soul, latching on to the crumpled body and the shadow memories. Its childlike attempt to run deep and hide only cemented itself to my soul. Always, it pushes at the bits, the pieces, to cover that it's here, inside me.

It . . . fear.

a Broken Cradle

Chapter 1

A Mother's Love

The room was dark, dimly lit by a lamp on the nightstand. I was on a bed lying on my stomach, naked. My twin brother was beside me, also naked. My mother, whom I never came to know, was standing over us. I remember that I was crying as she pushed a rod into my backside. At two, I didn't know or understand what was unfolding, and still am not sure. I do know that the memory is still here, and it marked the beginning—the journey of who I am.

My father, who was in the military and was gone most days, was unaware of the fact that we were left alone in the apartment often. This memory, as others, I see in black and white, like an old movie. The lack of color I'm sure has some significance that my mind filters at some point. I remember sitting on the floor, my brother beside me, in still silence. A diaper on each of us was our only piece of clothing. I can now only imagine how that moment, with all its miserable glory, influenced my existence and impressed my personality.

Anyone who reads the divorce papers will conclude that the military pushed my dad to divorce her. Dad met Marie while stationed in La Rochelle, France. She was working in the snack bar on base. They were married in November 1955 (he was twenty-two and she was twenty-seven). My sister was born on Christmas Day in 1956.

We came along in May 1958. When Dad found out she was pregnant with us, he shipped her back to the States to live with Grandma in Battle Creek, Michigan. He sent her back to the States so his tour wouldn't be extended as she would have been in her third trimester and couldn't travel. She kept stealing from Grandma's purse and shoplifting in town, so Grandma said she had to leave. She was taken in by our Uncle John. He lived in Palmyra, a little "blip" of a town. Boxes were barely cold from being unpacked when they realized that the stealing was still continuing. They spoke to her about it, she denied it, and for a while, it stopped. When the time came, they took her to Adrian (the closest hospital—Bixby Hospital), where she gave birth to us in 1958.

Dad came back from France when we were eight or nine weeks old.

His next military post was in Fort Riley, Kansas, where we spent eighteen months.

We then packed up and traveled to Nurnberg, Germany, his next post. It was here that we set our sister's bed on fire. My sister said that we—my twin and I—were sitting along the side of the bed with our backs touching it. We would light a match and throw it over our heads onto the bed. The match light would put out before hitting the bed—what are the odds . . . the mattress exploded into flames. My dad came running in from the other room, grabbed the mattress, and shoved it out of the window. He lined us up on the floor and blistered our behinds with his belt. I truly believe that when he said, "This is gonna hurt me more than it's gonna hurt you," he absolutely meant it. This was the first of only two times he ever hit me.

It was in Germany that Dany fell out of the window onto the sidewalk, tearing her scalp open. She was rushed to the hospital and stitched up. No one ever found out how she fell while being supervised by our mother, or whether our mother was there when it happened. No one seemed to know where our mother was. Dany was one year old then.

A few months later, my twin tripped and fell on the sidewalk and busted his chin open on a brick. It was pretty nasty. He has a permanent scar on his chin, which is how a lot of people tell us apart.

Germany had a lot of chimney sweeps. They all looked the same to us—all dressed in black, wearing tall, slender top hats, cleaning equipment strapped all over them, and really sooty. They looked like the boogeyman, and we were very terrified of them. Marie was aware of our fear and used it to her advantage. She would leave us in the car while she paraded around and tell us, "If you don't behave, the boogeyman will come and get you." We would huddle up in the car watching them walk by, thinking that one of them would reach into the car and grab us at any moment. She would be gone for several hours, and it seemed like an eternity to us. I had recurring nightmares all through my childhood where I'd be walking past a dark room and a hand with a sooty long arm would reach out from under the bed and pull me under.

While giving a deposition during my parents' divorce, a neighbor of ours summed up our lives in Germany. She described it as "pathetic." After reading her depositions, I could only agree . . .

Some statements in the depositions went like this:

"Mrs. Swain is a frequent inhabitant of almost every major Gasthaus in Nurnberg and Furth, and her conduct there is unbecoming. Mrs. Swain, while married to SP4 Swain, had dates and affairs with men. Her actions were basically the same. She came in, danced and got drank, then left when it closed with a man, usually a young GI" (William A. Dimmett, 1st Lt., 25 April 1961).

"We felt very sad about the children. Everyone here cared for them at one time or another. They were left alone, and mind you, they are still babies. They got dirty and it was pathetic the way they looked, like waifs, they were always hungry, unless some of us went down to feed them. She would often ask a neighbor to watch them and leave the keys without saying thank you or goodbye, or where she was going and how she could be reached. If the neighbors were not home, she would just leave them alone. She was very temperamental and often beat the children" (Mrs. Joanna Wentz, 20 April 1961, Nurnberg, Germany).

"Different men would come in taxis during the day to pick her up. She would leave in the morning and not come back until very late, even after her husband returned from work. On several occasions, she didn't even come home at all. Mr. Swain worked very hard to care for the children and the home. They asked for their father often. They never asked for their mother. When I finally got angry about feeding, watching, and washing the children, I approached her. She said she did not care anything about the children or her husband. What could I say then?" (Mrs. Erna Dietz, 20 April 1961).

This is Dad's deposition:

"This all started in June 1960. My wife asked if she could go to the movies with our upstairs neighbor. I told her yes because for a year or more she had been cooped up in the house with the kids and me. I thought it would be good for her to get out of the house for a few hours. So the first week, they went out twice; the next week, it was three nights. They would come home around

4

11:30 p.m. The third week, they went out three nights, coming home around midnight. The hours kept up through the month of July. On the first of August, the couple went on vacation for a month, and my wife continued to go out three nights a week, coming in around 12:30 a.m. She was dressing quite elaborately, and one night, I was sitting in the living room when I saw the car pull up and turn out the lights and sit there. I stepped outside to see why. When I stepped outside, the car door opened and my wife got out. When the door opened, I recognized the man inside. It was the German policeman who had investigated when my wife had lost her billfold. I asked her if she had been out with him, and she blew up arguing. I asked her when she was going to stop going out and stay home with me and the kids again. She said when the couple upstairs got back from vacation, they were moving to Frankfurt two weeks later, and would stop when the couple moved. I agreed to this; however, when the couple moved, she continued to go out. One night after that, we were listening to records and she started crying. She said that she had been going out with this gasoline truck driver, but it was over and she wouldn't go out with another man anymore. Things went fairly well until October 1960, when I found a letter she had written to a man named Eddy, telling him she wasn't married and that she was in love with him and wanted to marry him. I asked her to think of the kids and me, and she said to give her a month to forget him. I again agreed. Our anniversary came November 19, and she said she wanted to go out for a while. I didn't want to argue on our anniversary, so I let her go. She came in at four-thirty that morning. I again asked her when she was going to stop, and she said she would on the first of December. On November 30, she went out and was gone for four days. She said she had been seeing a musician for over a month and was in love with him. She said if I didn't leave her, she would stop. She went out New Year's Eve and was gone for three days and then went out January 5 and was gone until the seventh. I asked her to stop, and she said that she was in love with a man named Nico, but they had a fight and it was over. Around March 1961, she told me that she had been going out with a GI from Pinder Barracks and wanted a divorce. I told her that I wanted the kids, and she agreed. The first of April, she said he had been killed in an automobile accident and she was through with men. She said he was the man she loved and he was gone. That same week, she was seen in four different barracks. I went to one of the barracks, Merrell Barracks, and the guard told me that she had told everyone that I had been killed and she was seeing a GI named Eldrich. He told me she was there several nights a week. I went looking for her and found her in the Colibri Bar in Furth, dancing with a GI. I called home to the States and asked my parents for the money to get a divorce" (SP4 Myles E. Swain, 17 April 1961).

It's not easy, at any age, to accept that the woman who gave birth to you was a slut. We were doomed from the start . . .

When it came time for her deposition, two of the questions/answers hit home:

"Mrs. Swain, you realize that, not only are you an unfit mother and wife, but your undesirable actions, such as dating and having frequent intercourse with men not your husband, have made you a menace to the image of what should be true of an American dependent?"

"Yes, I feel that what I do is my business, so long as I do not break the law."

"Mrs. Swain, you do not desire custody of any of the children?"

"That is correct. I do not desire custody of the children."

My dad wanted to finalize the divorce in Europe but was eager to get rid of her, so after getting approval to end his tour early because of family crisis, he flew us back to the States in August 1961 to live with Uncle John in Palmyra. Marie stayed in Germany.

He finalized the divorce in the States.

Dad was next assigned to Fort Wayne in Detroit. He was commuting 150 miles a day so we could stay together. We weren't with Uncle John long when our uncle took a teaching job in Milan, so we packed our bags once again. Milan is about 30 miles northeast of Palmyra, and this added about 30 more miles to his commute. My brother and I shared a room with John, Helen's son. He slept in the bottom bunk, while my twin and I shared the top bunk. We could barely move around in that bed. We had to lie back-to-back and scrunch up to fit. Dany shared a room with Shila, Helen's daughter (let me add here that Helen had a hysterectomy when she was twenty-three, after having problems in two pregnancies). Dad slept on the sofa. Looking back now, I realize it had to have been difficult for Dad to do all that driving just to come home after a long day and sleep on a sofa, yet he did it day after day.

Things went okay for about a year. And during that year, Dad met Sylvia Fields. Tables were turned as she was nineteen and he was twenty-nine. Her parents were against them getting married because Dad was much older and had three kids, but in the summer of '62, they tied the knot.

That same year, he took an apartment in Detroit for Sylvia and himself. Dany and us twins would swap spending the weekends with them. I don't remember a lot about the apartment, except that it was hot, and I remember these hard candies with fruity, soft centers. They didn't live at the small apartment very long as he received orders to once again go to Germany. This time around, he would leave us behind with Aunt Helen. The reason for leaving us, we were told, was that the military discouraged families from bringing children overseas. But I think the real reason was that Dad's new wife, just being married, wanted to settle with her new husband before throwing his children into the mix. Think about it—a new husband, Germany, three kids—a lot of things for a nineteen-year-old to deal with. I mean, really, the children *are* the most dispensable, and with that, the fun began . . .

Chapter 2

If Not for the Love of an Aunt

I was always told that Aunt Helen really did want to keep us. Many of the memories about the time we lived with her, however, would solidly drive home the fact that she did not.

The moment Dad left, her personality changed—the gloves were off. Getting hit with a closed fist and being beaten was something that occurred almost daily. I remember having nosebleeds and bruises too numerous to count.

When we cried about what she did to us, it was "Shut up or I'll give you something to really cry about." I remember one occasion when I went outside to buy an ice cream from the ice cream truck that was driving down our street. For a nickel, you could get one of those ice creams on a stick that had a surprise inside when you got down to the center. I was really excited. As I came back inside the house, she swung, hitting me with such force I had a distinct feeling that I was flying through the air. It's like dreaming that you're falling and you never hit the ground. My hands were flailing about trying to grasp something. I went from standing in the doorway of the kitchen (leading out to the garage) to landing on the garage floor. I guess she didn't like the idea of me buying an ice cream. I was five then.

Another habit of hers was taping our mouths shut with a surgical adhesive tape when she thought we were talking too much. Once the tape was put on, it was there for the whole day. It would irritate the areas surrounding our mouths, and our lips would be chapped from licking the inside edges trying to loosen it. At the end of the day, she would rip it off in one fell swoop. Now, let that image settle into your brain . . . picture it in your mind. Can you feel it? I can. I remember the outline of the tape leaving a mark all the way around my mouth (as when you pull a Band-Aid off and there's a sticky, dirty outline). She would get rid of the sticky outline with lighter fluid. She always had a cigarette in her mouth, and I just knew that one day that cigarette was going to get too close to the lighter fluid. I knew this because she told me so.

Putting our hands over the stove burners set on high temperature was another form of torture she truly enjoyed and saved for the really special moments. She would turn the burner on, tightly grab hold of my wrist, and make me watch as the burner turned bright red. I think the anticipation of what was going to happen excited her. The sheer terror I felt really got her going and it was definite. No going back, no changing her mind. The tears running down our faces, the pleas to stop—like a television with the sound turned down. It didn't faze her. She held our hands about an inch or two over the center of the burner. We would try to pull away, jerking our hands several times, trying to loosen her grip. I thought when the pain had me close to passing out, she would stop. I was wrong. When she was done with one hand, she would repeat with the other. This was always done with the other twin watching. And just so the other one wouldn't get any ideas of misbehaving, he always got the same punishment, guilty or not. I would feel this throbbing pain for days and do my best to act as if nothing was wrong. It was difficult to come up with excuses to explain it away to people. To this day, because of that experience, I can hold hot things and not be bothered by the heat. It still, every single time, makes me remember of what I went through.

On many occasions, when we were going somewhere, she would "spot clean" our faces with her spit. She would take her hankie out, spit on it, and wipe our faces—mostly around our mouths. I still cringe thinking about the smell of her spit as she wiped it directly under my nose.

It was in our house in Milan that she would crack raw eggs over our heads. The eggs would run down our faces onto our shirts, but we weren't allowed to wipe them off. They would run into our eyes and ears, and they had to stay there until they had dried. I remember other people being there—her friends or high school friends of her children—and they were laughing at what she was doing to us. It was around this time that I started feeling I was an outcast.

I remember the sound of her voice as she called one of us into the bathroom. It was late—the house was quiet. We knew the drill. Get undressed and get into the bathtub . . . with her. The bathwater always seemed cloudy and dirty. I would get in and sit at the opposite end of the tub, her feet on either side of me. I would sit there, afraid to move, hoping that I was just dreaming the whole thing. *There were times when I couldn't tell the difference—dreaming and reality. I remember standing in front of the toilet, peeing, and then waking up in bed, soaked in urine (that happened a lot)* . If our gaze stayed in one spot for too long, she would grunt, "What in the hell are you looking at?" For the one waiting, it was the unbearable anguish and fear of what was about to happen. I think if I were born without a twin, I wouldn't have made it out alive. My twin and I depended on and used each other to get through. According to Dad, when we twins were younger, we would talk to each other without speaking—one of us would answer the other, without the other asking anything. I read, in my adult life, that it's common for twins to do that. Funny thing to remember, though, the bathwater so cloudy and dirty . . .

Milan is where we started kindergarten. We actually should have started a year earlier, but when Aunt Helen took us to register, the school explained that since our birthday was in May, we would have to wait until the following year. The first day of school, she walked us there to show us the way. It was about a mile. Day 2, we had to get there on our own—just me and my twin. We tried our best to find the school, but as you have probably guessed, we got lost. We finally stopped in this general store in town to ask a lady for directions, and she showed us where to go. We were actually only a few blocks away from the school the entire time we were trying to get there. We were quite late that day, and it took us several more tries before we could get there from memory. We told Aunt Helen about us getting lost, but she never helped us. We must have been told not to talk to strangers because we were always scared when someone would speak to us. We would speed up our walk home, looking back frequently to see if the person who spoke to us was following us.

I learned about the tooth fairy in kindergarten. I couldn't wait for one of my teeth to fall out. The day came when it did, and I was beside myself with anticipation of what was going to happen while I was asleep. I showed my tooth to everyone at school and at home. I put it under my pillow and lay in bed that night trying to guess what she looked like, and hoped that I would stay awake long enough to get a glimpse of the all-magical tooth fairy. I woke up the next morning and lifted my pillow . . . my tooth was still there. Did she forget? Was she too busy? This happened over and over and was repeated with my Christmas letter to Santa. I wrote a letter to Santa in hopes of getting that most prized treasure, "Rock 'em Sock 'em Robots," but I never found it under the tree. I told Santa that I had been a good boy all year, but I never found anything from my list under the tree. I thought I was the worst kid in the world if Santa didn't bring me a single present. We got presents from family and friends, but never from Santa. I remember getting this soap on a rope with a note that said, "From Santa," but I knew it was Shila's handwriting. I told everyone at school that Santa came to my house so that my friends wouldn't know that he passed me by.

Easter and Halloween were more of the same. We were dressed as hobos for our first Halloween. We even had a stick with a hobo bag tied to the end. By the end of the evening, we had our brown paper bags halfway filled with candies. We were beside ourselves with excitement and anticipation of the treasures in our bags. When we got home, Helen put our candies in a bowl and set the bowl up on a shelf in the kitchen. We weren't allowed to have any. We looked at that bowl full of candies every day knowing we weren't going to get any. Our Easter was just a repeat of Halloween. I wondered for many years what a chocolate rabbit tasted like.

I'm not sure if it was my fear of her or her lack of any love and nurturing that caused me to wet the bed on a regular basis. When asked by a neighbor why we weren't in school, Marie explained that we still wet our pants. I guess most parents teach their children with love and understanding and a high degree of tolerance. Not the case here, however.

Helen's ingenious method was to make us wear our pajama bottoms tied around our necks. We had to wear them the entire day, and sometimes overnight. We had to wear them wherever we went that day—with her to the grocery store, shopping, visiting her friends—anywhere that was populated and that struck her fancy. On her command, we had to pull our pajamas up to our noses and "smell" them, always "commanding" when people were around to see (it was more effective that way). If we delayed too long in doing it, she would grab them up, shove them into our faces, and hold them there.

Another part of the ritual was to endure sleeping on the same soiled sheets and pajamas for nights on end. This was going to "fix" the problem and break our bad habit.

Another torture she used was to make us "hold it" on long trips in the car. There were times when I thought I would pass out from the pain of my bladder. She threatened to wrap a rubber band around it if we didn't hold it. Sometimes she would pull the car over, and sometimes she wouldn't.

We would go to the lake house for the summer when school was over. I remember our room smelling really musty and damp from being empty all year. Getting ready for bed, I would turn over the sheets, and the pee stains from previous summer were still there. She hadn't changed the sheets. I would slide my feet under the covers, trying not to touch the stains. It was hopeless. I would grit my teeth and just get in. There aren't any words to explain exactly what that experience did to me emotionally, so I will leave it at that.

Uncle John and Helen were avid bowling fans. They were in a bowling league every Saturday night. Helen would practice her swing or throw in the living room on Saturday afternoons before going to the bowling alley. One particular afternoon, she had Mike and me line up side by side, about four feet apart (our backs to the wall). We were going to be her gutters. She did her walk-through over and over, stopping short of throwing the ball. I think it was on purpose that she let go of the ball. We both ducked and the ball hit the wall, leaving this big hole. Of course, she beat us for ducking, and Uncle John was mad about the hole. The hole stayed there the remainder of our stay in that house.

When we were living with Helen's family, they had a cat named Tony, a Great Dane named Alfie, and a terrier mix named Skippy. They took Tony to the vet to get fixed and found out that "he" was a "she." We came to love that cat. Anyway, we were eating dinner one night and Tony jumped up on the table. Helen hauled off and hit her, sending her flying off the table, landing on the kitchen floor, crying in pain, unable to get up. We found out later that her leg was dislocated and had to be reset.

They ended up giving Alfie away just before we moved to Webberville. He jumped on top of their car one evening and the roof caved in. It was one of those bubble top–looking Pontiacs. They told the insurance company that a tree fell on it.

Aunt Helen had one great love in her life: Skippy. She loved that dog more than anything. She doted on him, pampered him, and wherever she was, he was too. She ended up having that dog for twenty-three years. When he grew old, he became blind, deaf, ornery, and lost control of his bowels and bladder. He just kept holding on, and she kept holding on to him. Skippy had a stroke one day while he was outside, wandered into the street, and was hit by a car. I was long out of her influence then, but I guess she cried. One way of looking at this is, she treated her dog better than she did us, which speaks volumes. Don't get me wrong, I think everyone should treat their pets like they were their children— like part of the family. Helen just put her own little twist on it.

Chapter 3

Hell Has a House

*I*n 1965, Uncle John was offered a job as principal of a high school in Webberville, Michigan, and once again we packed up and moved. I always had this fear that moving around would make it hard for Dad to find us. What if he didn't know where we were? How was he going to rescue us? He called periodically, so my fears were always allayed. We could never tell him anything, as Helen was always right there beside us to listen to the conversation. Whenever we wrote letters to him, she would read them before mailing them. If something in the letter didn't meet her approval, we had to redo it. She always had us add in the letter that we were very happy living with them.

The house was large—a two-story old house that needed some "fixing up." It had three floors if you include the cellar. The size of the house meant no more cramping. My twin and I had our own room, Dany and Shila shared a room, Little John had his own room. Things were looking up.

We had bunk beds again. We would swap who slept where, as it didn't matter to us. Helen put heavy plastics on the mattresses because of the bed-wetting. The sheets would crinkle whenever I moved around on the bed. I couldn't explain it then, but that plastic made me feel embarrassed that it was put there. I was worried if one of my friends came over and went to my room, they would find out. Not to worry about it, however—our friends never came inside the house, which I now find odd. Was the word spreading about Helen and how she treated us? Did my friends' parents think we were bad kids? I'd be thinking about that for a while.

Within our first couple weeks, we would get up at night and pee in the closet next to our room because we were scared to go downstairs to the bathroom—afraid of the dark, afraid we would disturb Helen—something we learned to try not to do. The bathroom was also far from our bedroom and some distance to go—in the dark when you're a kid. There was only one bathroom in the house. It was on the main floor at the rear of the house by the back door and cellar. We would have to pass right by her bedroom to get there. Eventually, everything in the closet started to smell like pee. She found out about it, and we got one of the most severe beatings we'd ever had. Blow after blow—fists, belts, anything that she knew would hurt—was sent our way. And it wasn't immediately distributed. It was very methodical. She would concentrate on one area at a time, hitting the same spot in my head several times, then moving to the arm for several blows, then to the back. I felt dizzy, and my eyes couldn't focus—a kind of feeling you have when you black out and come to. While one of us twins was being beaten, the other had to stand and watch so he would know what was going to happen to him when she was done with the first twin. Everything in the closet had to be thrown out. The closet walls and floor were made of wood, so the smell never did completely go away. The bed-wetting would continue until we were nine or ten.

The bathroom was quite small for a large house. Helen would have us wash up in the sink. All three of us had to stand around

17

the sink and wash up together and use the same washcloth and water as much as the sink could fill. So here we were, the three of us, washing from head to toe, in one sink of water. On several occasions, we tried to drain the water and fill the sink with fresh water, but Helen would hear the water going down the drain and blow a gasket. Let me just say that we rarely took baths. Most of the time, standing around the sink was the closest we got to a bath. And it wasn't a nightly occurrence. If we were lucky, we would stand around the sink twice a week. We would pour some of Uncle John's Old Spice aftershave in the water when it got murky. Every now and then, we would pour some talcum powder in the water, but it didn't mix well. It floated on top of the water and made bubbles when we would turn the water on. It stuck to the washcloth and ended up being more of a mess than it did helping our cause. A lot of times, after we cleaned up, she would call us into the living room to clean our ears. She didn't do this with a cotton swab; she did this with a bobby pin. Helen would shove that bobby pin down into our ears and scrape it around the ear canal. It was very painful, and sometimes our ears would bleed. Funny thing . . . cotton swabs were always in the bathroom.

Webberville is where we had our first grade. Since it was a small town, my twin and I were quite popular with the other kids. We were the only twins in that small town. I had my first girlfriend in Ms. Haight's first-grade class. She was a pretty little blonde named Lynnette Vorce. I would give her rings that I got out of the bubble gum machine all the time. We went steady until the fourth grade. My brother also had a steady girlfriend until fourth grade—Terry Bohnett. We completely separated our school life from our home life. We did our best to forget the situation at home. School became a sanctuary—a place where we could pretend home didn't exist. It was picture-perfect—like one that Norman Rockwell painted. Nothing bad happened at school. It was always the opposite. I so loved my school world. I was always one of the first to be picked for kickball, dodge ball, red rover, or whatever game we were playing. Thinking about it now, I realize I was in that small group of popular "in" kids. Nowadays, they call such groups "cliques." This was the only time in my life that I was part of one. In a lot of ways, my school life in Webberville was the happiest time of my life. It's one of those memories that, when you look back, always bring me a smile. I learned in school that I had an artistic talent—all that emotion had to go somewhere. I was quite good at drawing and sketching; my classmates would have me draw stuff like horses and cartoon characters for them. My fond of drawing grew into a love of painting, and I eventually grew up selling several paintings. This talent has stayed with me my whole life.

Our posse or gang consisted of me, my brother, Jeff Chase, Eugene Haywood, and Tom Hodges. We were in the same class, together in Cub Scouts, and we were always doing something as a group. Whenever my brother and I could get away from home, we would find them. Most of the time, people would see three or four of us doing something together. We were inseparable. Something our friends did for us was making the pain seem not so bad. We were becoming numb to the pain anyway. I think a person stops feeling the pain after a certain point—when he gets it on a regular basis, he tends to expect what's coming.

Just after moving to Webberville, we went to the hospital to have our tonsils and adenoids taken out for the second time. Through most of our childhood, my twin and I always seemed to have the same things happen to us at the same time—tonsillitis, mumps, measles, chicken pox, etc. . . . We had to have tubes put in our ears twice to try to stop all our earaches. Grandma got teddy bears for both of us to take to the hospital to keep us company. We were there for about three days, and when we went home, I realized that I had left my teddy behind. I told Aunt Helen and she said, "Well, you shouldn't have left it." Unknown to me at the time, about a week later, a letter from the hospital came, informing her that they had my teddy and we could come pick it up. She had thirty days to make arrangements. The hospital wasn't that far away, but she never made arrangements to go and get it. This one small gesture was surely not so much to ask. Thirty minutes to drive round-trip to do one nice thing. It broke my heart not getting my teddy back. Like me, he was discarded—not worthy of some time. My brother managed to keep his into adulthood. I was glad that he had his, but it was a constant reminder that I didn't have mine.

It was a routine: She would clean the house, starting on the bottom floor, working her way up the stairs. She would get to my sister's room first, which was always in order (probably out of fear). We had to wait in our room until she was done. We could hear when she was on her way down the hall to our room. The fear of what was going to happen was unbearable. Whenever she found anything out of order or not in its place, we were slapped, or hit upside the head, or pushed to the floor. On really bad days, we got the belt, or, as she called it, "the Board of Education." It was a thick paddle with holes drilled in it to cut through the wind easier. On the front was painted Board of Education. I remember changing clothes at school for gym class and the other boys making fun of me because my butt was bruised and bloodied from the beatings. Sometimes up to three-fourths of my butt was covered with the bruises.

I guess the fear on this day was too much to handle. My brother and I climbed outside to the roof of the second story of the house to hide from her. The ground was covered with about two feet of snow. My sister was on the ground outside egging us on to jump, saying that the snow would break our fall. Since the roof was nine or ten feet from the ground, I couldn't deduce that the snow wouldn't break my fall, so I jumped thinking that it would. We were to jump at the count of three. On three, I jumped—he didn't. Relieved that I wasn't dead, I lay there, in the snow, pain starting to run up my leg. I had broken my foot. When Helen saw me later that day limping, I told her that I fell down the stairs, which she bought. She said, "I thought I heard something this morning . . . that must have been it." That same evening, we had to go buy school clothes and shoes. I remember how bad the pain was as she forced a shoe onto my swollen foot. I told myself that she probably forgot that my foot was hurt, but she didn't forget.

I'm not sure what prompted it, but on one occasion, she was blaming something on us. We were denying it, so she made us both sit in chairs and told us we were going to sit there all night until we admitted whatever it was. Of course, we had to forgo dinner. After about an hour, we started getting sleepy. Just as I was nodding off, she walked by and slapped me in the face. I tried to stay awake, but I nodded off again. She slapped me again to wake me up. After a couple of hours, she had us pull our pants down every hour and hit us with the paddle full of holes. She finally gave up about four in the morning and sent us to bed. It was the only time she ever gave up, and it was clearly not a victory for us.

The next day, we waited for the bomb to drop, but nothing happened. We went to Cub Scouts that night and we were having our usual good time with the gang. Our troop leader's phone rang. She answered it, spoke with the person on the other end, and hung up. She looked as though something was wrong as she came over to us and said that the person on the phone was Aunt Helen (really, she said it was our mother). Helen informed her that we would have to quit the Scouts but didn't give her a reason. Along with our troop leader, we were heartbroken. We now knew the reason she gave up the previous evening. She was plotting something bigger, and better. Helen knew that we loved the Scouts more than anything, and she was hammering in the stake extra deep this time. On our way home that night, we twins talked about running away. We even plotted for a few days, but our courage dwindled and faded away. As the idea of running away was abandoned and forgotten, extreme hatred for Helen surfaced. We hated her already, but this time it was different. It went way deep inside. We wanted her to die.

Uncle John was a principal in charge of several hundred students. He was hired to look out for their best interest, their safety, yet he didn't see or realize what was happening to us in his own house. I knew there were a lot of clues, most of which we had on our bodies. I saw it in my brother's face every time I looked at him. I saw the beaten-down, hopeless look of desperation that permeated from his eyes, as though a part of him was gone. And I knew he saw the same in mine. I find that whole scenario a bit ironic.

I don't remember Uncle John being affectionate to us. He was never mean or anything like it; he just didn't show affection. I do remember him bringing home boxes of potato chips and snacks—the ones that fit into the vending machines at school. He would bring home plain chips, barbecue chips, cheese crackers, and popcorn. At the time, it seemed special that he did that, like an unexpected present. And on one occasion, he did let us go to summer camp for a week. We stayed in cabins, and the whole gang was there. The camp had archery, crafts, marshmallow roasts, trails in the woods, and swimming. It is one of the very few happy memories of my childhood. Before camp started, we had to get some new boots. We picked out these neat green boots with beige trimming. They were what everyone else in our gang had. Aunt Helen picked out these crappy black galoshes with metal clamps on them. I remember Uncle John telling her to let us get what we wanted. We were so excited to get them and, for once, be like everyone else. I loved Uncle John for letting us have that memory.

Being principal kept him at school a lot. He had to attend all the home games, away games, staff meetings, special events and functions, and on a lot of weekends, he went hunting. I do remember him being home most evenings before we went to bed. Looking back, I realize he and Helen never really seemed that close or loving to each other. I don't even recall ever seeing them kiss in front of us. We never heard them argue and never saw them fight; they just weren't the touchy-feely type of people. Maybe that explains why in 1969, we found out that he had been seeing one of his senior students at the high school. He was balding, only had hair on the sides and back of his head, but when he started seeing the student, he got a hair transplant. He also lost weight—I guess it was his "change of life." He had evidently been seeing her for quite a while. He asked Helen for a divorce the following year and, yes, ended up marrying the student. They were together the remainder of his life. I believe that Cheri was the love of his life. During their marriage, they became parents— of twin boys. Uncle John passed away in 2003.

Chapter 4

Childhood Lost

Growing up in the late '50s and '60s, what happened in a family stayed in the family. No one from the outside got involved, or spoke out, even when they witnessed something firsthand. Seriously, you could practically beat your kids to death in front of a crowd of people and they wouldn't bat an eye. So I always thought that what was happening to us was normal for every family. Nonetheless, I was always insecure and embarrassed when around people, thinking they would look at me and know what had happened. And I felt as though everyone we knew thought of us as "bad kids." Helen probably set it up that way.

When school was over, we would go to the lake for the duration of the summer. They had a vacation house that sat on a lake near Coldwater, Michigan, a couple of hours from home. It was a very rural, country town—one that everyone writes about and you always see in movies. What we always hoped to enjoy on a great summer, such as fishing; catching frogs, crickets, and night crawlers; picking blackberries—all the things little boys did on a summer break—would end up miserably painful. Whenever we had the chance, we would walk the dirt road to the general store and buy a soda or candy. We loved cream soda in a bottle. Our favorite things to buy were Cracker Jacks, candy necklaces, Black Jacks (they don't make them anymore; I would love to find some), and Clove gum. We would daydream all the way back home, stopping along the way to play. Sometimes we would take the rowboat out and fish. We would row out to the sandbar in the middle of the lake. You could actually get off the boat and walk around in the middle of the lake. That was a lot of fun.

Most mornings Helen would wake us up before it was daylight, feed us, and take us to the dreaded garden up the road where we had to pull weeds all day long—God, I hated it! It was always hot, the bugs would swarm from the sweat, and there were a lot of snakes. The tomato plants always had huge green tomato worms that we were scared of. They looked like giant caterpillars with spikes sticking out of them, so why they call them worms, I have no idea. Pulling weed after weed after weed was truly tedious and disgusting. To pass the time, we would talk to the bobwhites. They are birds that are common in the area. We would say out loud, "Bob bobwhite," and within a few seconds, one of them would respond by chirping three times, which sounded like bob bobwhite. It was really cool.

One weekend (we were six years old), she decided that she was going to teach us to swim. Up to this point, we would generally splash and wade in the shallow part of the shore next to the dock. She called us out of the water and onto the dock. She told us of her plan. I can still feel the fear that instantly took us over. She explained the schematics of swimming, had us stand on the edge of the dock near the deep end, and pushed us off. Her philosophy was to have us either swim or drown. My hands were grabbing at the water, but cutting right through. I was trying to catch my breath and kept swallowing dirty lake water. She repeated this several times before letting us stop. She told us we would do it again the next day, and she kept her word, and we did it in the next several days. One of the more horrifying moments of my life.

Later that first day, she took us to the general store to get ice cream (I thought she was trying to make up for the swimming lesson). She asked us what we wanted and went inside to get them while we waited in the car. She came back to the car, already eating hers. It wasn't until we were driving away that we realized she didn't buy any for us.

It was during our trip to the lake when school was off or our trip back home at the end of summer that the "bitch" told us we had to start calling her "mother." Now, we knew she wasn't our mother, and she wasn't someone I wanted to call mother—it just wasn't right, it just didn't fit, but we knew if we didn't, the Wrath of Helen would be upon us. So from that point on, we did. I do have to say, calling her mother only instilled the notion that we would probably be spending the rest of our lives in hell.

As I stated before, during the year, my uncle would work at the high school in Webberville. During the summer, he would build houses in Coldwater, where we spent the summers. He would go to Wicks, the lumberyard, for supplies and take us with him. We loved that place. They had this big barrel of salted peanuts in the shell at the front of the store, and we would stuff ourselves.

One day, Uncle John sent Helen to Wicks in his place to pick up a few things, and we were told to ride along. We arrived and headed for the peanut barrel. She reminded us, as she always did, to behave or else. I'm not sure if we acted up (we didn't think we did). After some time, we decided to go look for her. We couldn't find her anywhere. We went to the parking lot and the car was gone. We sat down and started crying. We felt abandoned . . . on our own. I remember thinking that we were going to be in trouble for getting left behind, for her leaving without us—funny how one processes information. After about thirty minutes, she showed up. "Maybe next time you'll listen when I say something!" I think she was hoping that someone had taken us.

Many times, it was up to us to fill most of our days. Since she didn't care about us, she rarely kept up with us and our whereabouts. There was no teaching us, no helping us learn right from wrong. It was only when we were getting underfoot that we got punished, and it was only then that we knew what "wrong" was. We were held accountable for the lack of supervision she gave us. We tried to avoid her as much as possible.

Once Aunt Helen was visiting one of her friends, Dora Haynes, who lived up the road. Dora and her husband, Max, owned the property that Uncle John had built the lake house on. They owned a big chunk of the property in the area, but if you looked at them, you would never guess they were wealthy. Max wore overalls most of the time, and Dora always had a day dress on. They were good, down-to-earth people who lived modestly, and they were quite nice and caring to us. Until "Auntie" was through visiting and ready to leave, it was up to us to amuse ourselves. Their farm had this huge barn on the property, and we would hang out there—all kinds of neat things around a barn when you're a little kid. We climbed up to the loft and played a while, throwing clumps of hay at the bats in the rafters. Then we played hide-and-seek and topped the afternoon off with some exploring.

Out behind the barn was this huge pile of junk metal. It was just metal or garbage to most people, but to us it was a treasure trove. Amidst the pile was this broken old wooden cradle. It was weathered, and weeds were growing around it. There was sadness lingering around it, and I felt it. I walked over to it. Next to the cradle on the ground was a dirty, also weathered baby's pacifier. Only from a child's mind, but I picked it up and put it in my pocket so it wouldn't get cold.

We came across a swing blade propped up against the side barn. We weren't sure what it was but figured it out rather quickly. My brother swung it at the tall weeds, and we were amazed at how easy it cut things. I told him that I wanted to take my turn swinging it, but he wasn't ready to give it up. I tried to approach him to take it away, but he kept swinging it at me to keep me away. I made a mad dash for it and it caught me in the eye, just under my eyebrow. Blood was gushing. I thought I was going to die, and so I ran to the house, screaming all the way. Helen and Dora came out to see what was going on, saw the blood, and took me into the house. Once inside, Dora cleaned me up and said it looked like I needed stitches. It was a pretty nasty gash, but Helen had this look in her eyes that said I had totally ruined her day and she was pissed. I wasn't taken to the hospital. Instead, she put tincture of iodine on it, bandaged it, and called it a day. My brother got a nasty beating to match the nasty cut on my eye.

Same summer, same scenario—just replace the swing blade with a burn barrel. We had a fifty-five-gallon drum in the front yard that we used to burn garbage. We were throwing garbage in and watching the flames shoot up over the top of the barrel. I decided to throw a foam pillow in, which stoked the fire. Pieces of the burning pillow were flying up in the air, and a piece came down, landing on my forearm. It instantly burned my skin, which caused me to run around in circles screaming, shaking my arm to remove it, but it was glued to my skin. We ran to the hose, turned it on, aimed it at my arm, and let the water cool the foam. I tell you, it hurt like a mother. I got a third-degree burn, and she didn't take me to the doctor. She did nothing. This huge blister grew on my arm, and she didn't take me to the doctor. She did nothing. I have a scar on my arm to this day, as a reminder in case I forget. I thought the lack of medical attention was punishment for being bad, but the truth of the matter was she didn't want any proof— nothing documenting all the injuries, all the bruises, all the cuts, all the broken bones, all the burns—did I leave anything out?

Her favorite color was red—go figure. I told her that my favorite color was also red, thinking if I had the same favorite as she, maybe she would back off a little bit. It didn't help. Nothing helped when she made up her mind.

So, Helen, if you can hear me down there, my favorite color isn't red. Never has been. My favorite color is grey. Did you hear me? *Grey!*

A few weeks later, she went out for a while and returned with some live chickens. We thought, *Oh boy, we have chickens to play with!* She unloaded the crates one by one, hanging the chickens upside down with their legs attached to the clothesline in the backyard. Methodically, one by one, she slit their throats with a razor blade. They were flapping around, clucking, and blood was spraying all over them and on to the ground. I literally froze in horror. One chicken got loose from the rope before she got to it. It took off running, and she made us go after it. We were chasing it, but shooing it away at the same time, hoping it would run away. It ran into the woods, and after some time, she told us to forget it and come back. We were happy that our ill attempt to catch it aided its escape.

We came back to where she was in the backyard, and she was already beheading them, gutting them, and pulling the feathers off. Once she had dressed them, she gave us the dead bodies to pull all the pinfeathers off. Pulling pinfeathers off a chicken is very difficult, as your hands get slimy after a while, making it difficult to pull them, and they are burrowed into the skin. We would get hold of one feather and pull over and over 'til it finally came loose. The ordeal took a couple of hours to finish, and the smell was starting to get to us—the pile of "innards" was right beside us. Well, needless to say, we had chicken that night for dinner. We also had homemade bread.

One nice thing I can say about Helen is she could make some bread from scratch. She made the best toast. The house always smelled so good during bread-making time. She was well-known in town for her bread. She would give out loaves as gifts during Christmas. On bread-making days, she would have the entire kitchen filled with pans of rising dough. It was everywhere. It had to rise twice. During the leavening process, we weren't allowed anywhere near the kitchen. She would give her usual "or else" threat to warn us. Well, lo and behold, the bread fell. Now, we weren't anywhere near that kitchen—must have been our telekinetic powers at work. Needless to say, we were blamed and punished. This time, she had our heads shaved. I spent most of my childhood with a shaved head.

Chapter 5

Merry Christmas

*I*t was Winter 1969. We were in the family room watching TV. *Dark Shadows* was on, and as usual, we were glued to the screen. It was a weekly soap opera about a family of vampires. Barnabas Collins was the main vampire. Kate Jackson, in one of her first roles, played Daphne. It was really scary for kids our age, and everyone at school watched it. The phone was ringing, but we paid no mind. Aunt Helen answered it, and again, we didn't give it much thought. After she hung up the phone, she came in to where we were. I'll never forget this: she said, "That was your dad, and he wants you to come live with him. When we go down for Christmas, you'll be staying. Dany, you have a choice. You can stay here with us if you want, but you boys *are going.*" Dany said she wanted to go with us and live with Dad. Helen said okay.

Was it really over? Were we dreaming? Maybe this was another cruel joke at our expense. What if she changed her mind? We tried our best to not make her mad at us (like she really needed a reason) so she wouldn't. From that point until we left, nothing bad happened. We figured she didn't want us going home with noticeable bruises or cuts.

We left school for Christmas break. I can still see myself crying miserably as I said goodbye to my best friends. I told myself that when I grew older, I would come back and see them, and we would once again be best friends. I was also leaving my steady girlfriend in the last four years. I called her on the phone and asked her to marry me when she grew up. She said, "I have to take my piano lesson now."

We packed the station wagon and started for North Carolina. Maybe this was really going to happen after all. It was a sixteen- to eighteen-hour-drive—plenty of time for them to change their minds. We felt a lot better once we pulled into the driveway and saw Daddy. We saw our little brother, Sean, born October 30, 1968, for the first time. And I have to say, the next few days were the best that I had ever felt or experienced to that point. It was the kind of Christmas that you read about in storybooks. It was the Christmas that every child dreams of, that I dreamed of every year of my life. We weren't home free yet as Helen was still here.

At the end of the week, they packed up, said their goodbyes, and got into the station wagon. The last look Helen gave me seemed to be one of anger. I initially thought she was angry knowing we wanted to stay with Dad; she had no control over us anymore. Over time, I came to realize that she was angry because she was going back home without us as her outlets. She had no one to vent to, let her frustrations out on, unleash her anger on. I have often wondered about the days after she got home and what it was like for her.

I vividly remember watching the station wagon pull out of the driveway and drive down the street. My eyes didn't look away until I saw the taillights disappear. The whole time it was driving away, I kept thinking it was going to turn around and come back, come back and get us. It didn't. We had escaped. There aren't words to describe . . .

Helen would pass away in 1993. I didn't go.

The next few days were like a dream. We were that storybook family you read about where the parents tuck you in at night and kiss you instead of giving you a nosebleed or a board across your butt.

After the Christmas holiday, we registered at our new school. I remember feeling like an outcast—coming in to the classroom after half the year was gone. Being the new kid in class isn't fun. Everyone has already picked their friends, and no one has room for one more. I felt invisible for the remainder of the fourth grade. They changed the school districts by summer, so most of the kids were scrambled as to which school they went. I wouldn't be the only new kid anymore. The school was new to all the kids, many of them losing their friends.

Fifth grade was a good year for me. I made friends, had a girlfriend, and was voted class president. My being class president was short-lived—I got in trouble in a horseplay in the bathroom and was dethroned. I had disappointed my teacher, and that made me feel awful. I didn't want her to see me in a bad light. When I became the spelling bee champion, I was back in her good graces. No one could beat me. I won against everyone they put me up against. Whenever they put us in teams, everyone wanted to be on my team as they knew I would be victorious.

My girlfriend, Kristin Simpson, was the prettiest girl in the class. I wrote her one of those classic notes: I like you, do you like me? Check yes or no. She said yes. Every other week, I would give her a necklace or a ring. We went steady for the whole school year. Fifth grade turned out to be the best year I would ever have in school.

Life at home was moving along well. Our new mom was very attractive—she was definitely a "looker." When Mom would come to school for one reason or another, the kids would say, "Dang, your mom is hot!" She gave me a bit of notoriety with my classmates.

One thing that stood out at home was how my twin was behaving. He was frequently getting into trouble. It was petty stuff most of the time, but in seventh grade, it got out of hand. Dad had been sent overseas to Korea. Mom was finding it difficult working a full-time job and caring for us without the help of Dad. She worked overtime quite a bit, and it was up to us to keep things going at home and watch over our younger brother. Mom would pay us a weekly allowance for doing our chores and watching over Sean. My twin and Dany didn't really like watching over him, so I would take the weeks they were scheduled to babysit and they would give me their allowance.

We came home after school one day to find that our house had been broken into. We called Mom, who in turn called the police. The police looked around, asking us to look for anything that might be missing. A couple of shotguns and several coins from Dad's collection were the only things missing. The police officer told Mom that the robbery looked staged. By the time it was over, my twin admitted it was him but wouldn't tell anyone why he had done it. With the help of the military, Mom contacted Dad, who was allowed to come home on an emergency leave. I guess they thought Dad could talk some sense into my twin. Dad was home about two weeks and left again. His trip home didn't have the impact they were expecting. My twin's stealing continued from seventh grade all the way through the end of high school. He forged our little brother's documents at the bank, wiping out his savings account. He stole several credit cards from Mom and Dad and used them to withdraw cash on ATMs. On the day of our high school graduation, Mom and Dad discovered more credit cards Michael stole. Their response was to pull him from the graduation ceremony. He had to sit with them and watch everyone else get their diplomas. The principal called his name, and everyone looked at me, wanting to know what was happening. All I could do was stand there and wait for them to call my name next. It was a very awkward moment. I'm not a mental health professional but would venture a guess that everything we went through up to now had taken a toll on my brother. This was also the point where we began to become distant from each other. We were moving into different paths. We each were finding a different set of friends, having separate interests, and it would never be the same between us. Other than looking identical, we would no longer be twins.

Another thing that stood out at home was how Mom treated Sean very differently than us. He was the golden child and did no wrong—ever. He always got the best, and we got whatever was left. We were the stepchildren, and while she didn't say it, her actions constantly let us know it. I didn't blame anyone—I loved them, but it still affected me; it affected all three of us. I didn't understand why she was like that until I was older, until I was in the same situation as her.

I love my little brother dearly, but Sean knew he was the golden child. He would pull it out of his pocket every time he wanted his way. He would say, "I'm gonna tell Mom on you," or, "I'll tell Mom you hit me if you don't let me have it." Him getting hit or punched didn't happen frequently, but Mom would always believe him more than anyone else. We learned to give him what he wanted in order to shut him up. We tested him a time or two by saying no, and Sean would holler, "Mom!" He would quickly get his way and then, smiling, cancel the call for help by saying, "Never mind."

Junior high was when I was made to feel uncomfortable around my peers in school. Junior high was eighth and ninth grades. Guys in both grades found it necessary to single me out as one whose life was going to be a living hell. I never figured out why I was the lucky one. Maybe it was because I didn't play any sports. Maybe it was because I wasn't very outgoing. Maybe it was because I didn't exude enough testosterone like the jocks. Most of my friends were girls—maybe that was it. Maybe I was guilty by disassociation. I was quiet, always had good grades, and was known for being artistic.

It all started out with one or two jocks making passing comments once in a while. Then it became more and more frequent with more guys jumping on the bandwagon. Before long, it became a full-blown witch hunt.

I had girlfriends in junior high and high school, but these relationships were short-lived. I think they got frustrated with or embarrassed by the people making comments and calling me names. It got to me, so I knew it affected them as well. I don't blame them—that time I was trying to find myself, searching for who I was, and the other students were trying to make me become what they were calling me. It probably played out in their heads like this: He's gonna be a faggot, so let's make fun of him, let's call him names, let's embarrass him and ruin his high school experience. Yeah, that will make us feel better about ourselves . . . that's what we'll do.

It worked. My life at school was hell. I couldn't walk down a single hallway a good part of the time without someone shouting some negative comment or word in my direction. And riding on the bus was just as bad. Most people didn't want to sit beside me, and instead would sit behind me and poke me, or pull my hair. There was the constant verbal threat to kick my ass.

Needless to say, while sorting things out and coming to terms with the fact that I was gay, I poured myself into my schoolwork. I managed to keep straight As throughout high school—that "always wanting to be the best" thing stayed by my side. I became friends with Millard in my ninth-grade Spanish class. He was a slightly nerdy only child of elderly parents. We had several classes together, but it was in Spanish class that we bonded. We were both very competitive, always trying to outdo each other by getting the best grade in class. At the end of the year, on the last day of school, the teachers gave out awards for best academic performance. My Spanish teacher, Ms. Barnhill, awarded me the best in Spanish award, but called Millard up as well. I had eked out a one-grade-point lead with a 103 average for the year.

My tenth-grade history class was where I met Ernie. He was popular and good-looking but didn't have a lot of close friends. He was somewhat of a loner, a rebel if you will, who didn't care what people think about what he said, and was very opinionated. His hair was longer than the norm, jet-black, and had these striking dark brown eyes. He wore blue jeans and a jean jacket most of the time. He was so cool. It surprised me that we became friends, with people talking about me the way they did, but Ernie didn't seem to care about that. He did his own thing. Academically, he was in the top ten. I graduated eighth out of 450 students in the senior class with a 95.05 average. I even missed twenty-nine days in a row my senior year. If you miss thirty days, they would hold you back from graduating. I thought I had more important things to worry about at the time, and my grades slipped during this period of "growing up."

I couldn't take the situation at home anymore. Upon finding out about my sexual preference—my brother "outed" me to my family and the people at school—Mom made things difficult for me at home. She made me stop all after-school activities—school clubs, games, etc. I was to go to school and directly come home and not leave the house until she got home. If she went somewhere, she took me with her. I was basically on house arrest. All this was supposed to correct the problem. It was going to make me see the light and decide I wasn't gay after all. The only thing Dad said about the whole situation was, "Well, we've never had one in the family before," and he left it at that. I think him saying that was his way of trying to make it easier on me—making the situation less dramatic. On that day, he was being a dad. I knew that it bothered him finding out his eldest son was queer. I knew he was disappointed.

Mom, on the other hand, was disgusted by the sight of me, and I was disgusted by her treatment of me; so while she and Dad were at work, I moved out. Hey, I was eighteen. I was calling the shots now. I knew best. Those twenty-nine days were the most broke, hungriest, most humbling days of my life. On day 29, I called my parents and asked them if I could come back home. That was a difficult phone call to make—I was wondering if it would be a yes or a no. It was a yes, and I was relieved. I went to school the next day and found out that if I had missed one more day, I would have failed. Go figure.

During this period of turmoil at home—before and after as well—I, with a few gay friends, would meet outside school, drive up to Raleigh on weekends, and party at the bars. I would start to get excited on Monday, looking forward to Saturday night. I couldn't wait to get back to Raleigh, and the sounds of ABBA, Thelma Houston, and Grace Jones. My "coming out" song (everybody has one) was "Dancing Queen" by ABBA (damn, I love that song). For those who aren't aware, a "coming out" song is the one that was playing at the bar the first night you were there, officially coming out of the closet. I have to say, I was totally petrified my first night in a bar. *All these men in here are gay? They're like me? What am I supposed to do in here?* My friends were more than willing to show me the ropes. And I have to say, I learned fast. A couple of cocktails and off I went. I would sometimes come back home with a hickey or two on my neck. I would switch names when telling people who put them there—if Al put it there, I would say Amy did. If Tommy did it, I would say Tammy did, and so on.

I couldn't write this book without mentioning Rocky. That was his real name. I met him while I was working at the mall when I moved out of my parents' house. Rocky played a key role in showing me the ropes and helping me come to terms with my being gay. We were the same age, and he had been "out" for several years already. In a lot of ways, he saved my life during a very emotional period. He was there for all my firsts—first gay bar, first dance, first drunk, first date, and so on. We were pretty inseparable, and I will always remember him.

It was during this twenty-nine-day hiatus that my two best friends found out that I was gay. They found out indirectly through my brother. Upon my return to school, Ernie and Millard would have nothing more to do with me. I tried to deny it, but the truth had come out too far for me to try to stop it with a lie. Both had wanted to be my roommate in college, and I had planned on rooming with Ernie but hadn't figured out yet how to tell Millard. That would now fall by the wayside, as Ernie and Millard would become roommates.

The last several months of my senior year were miserable. My two best friends were gone, and word was getting around about me being a sissy. I have to say, I could have endured it, endured all the talk, all the comments and whispering, the embarrassment and isolation, endured it all if Ernie and Millard had stayed by my side. If they had decided that our friendship was worth the trials, then so many years of my life after that would have somehow been different. I can't help but believe that—'cause there have been so many times in the years after when I have told myself that—the two of them leaving changed something in me. I was no longer the same person inside. I was damaged goods, so to speak, and I would carry that change for most of my life. It would be the biggest hurt I would ever feel, the worst letdown I would ever know.

So now that I've said that, Ernie did come back into my life, briefly, during our last two weeks in school. I was glad as hell that he was back; it was just a bit perplexing at first. He walked up to me one day during graduation rehearsal and just started talking, as if nothing had happened. I don't know if he thought about things and had a change of heart—he never explained. I never asked; why take a risk and mess things up again? I think the real reason he rekindled our friendship those last few weeks was so that we could end things on a good note—part ways and move on with life without any bad feelings or regrets.

I smoked my first joint with Ernie. It was during our junior year. He and I had gone to see Lynard Skynard in a concert. Mother's Finest was the warm-up band. On our way to the auditorium, we smoked a couple of "doobies." He gave me a shotgun toke—it is done by holding the joint with the lit part inside your mouth and blowing the smoke out to the other person. Your lips are so close to the other person's, almost kissing—and I got mine as close as humanly possible to his. I figured if they touched, I could chalk it up to accident or being high. The world was fine that night.

For a brief moment, Ernie made me feel like I was cool. I was so stoned by the end of the concert—people were passing joints around all over the place. I could barely walk, so Ernie put his arm around me to prop me up and helped me walk out past the security officers. Midway to the car, I leaned my head on Ernie's shoulder, expecting him to move it off. He let me leave it there. I think that was the night I fell in love with him.

Later that year, in the fall, the three of us—Ernie, Millard, and me—drove up to UNC at Chapel Hill, the school we all wanted to go to. The weekend we drove up was beautiful. It was sweater weather—the air was colder, the leaves were changing colors and collecting on the ground, and the road to the campus was lined with an artist's palette of trees. The view was stunningly breathtaking. "Please Come to Boston" by Dave Loggins, "Fire and Rain" by James Taylor, "More Than a Feeling" by Boston played on the radio during our drive up. We also listened to some songs of Peter Frampton, Kiss, America, and Chicago. The music, the scenery, the windows rolled down, being seniors, the chill in the air . . . again, all was well with the world.

This was the first time any of us had been here, and it met all our expectations. I'd never seen the three of us more excited than at that moment. We booked a room for overnight at the campus inn. After dinner, a few beers, and a walk around the campus, we went to our room at the inn. Three people, two beds—do the math. What I was hoping would happen did. Ernie came out of the bathroom with his shirt off, and he was barefooted—he still had his pants on. He walked over to one of the beds and plopped down on his back. If I had any doubts, it was definitely now etched in stone. Seeing him lie there was such a beautiful moment for me. I wished Millard wasn't there in the room. Nothing would have happened, but my beautiful moment would have been so much better if it was just me and Ernie. I had to keep myself from staring. I certainly wasn't anywhere near ready for him or Millard to know how I felt. It would be an ongoing struggle that year, inside me, wanting with all my heart to tell Ernie but knowing I never would. We cut up a bit longer and finally went to bed. Millard slept by himself.

Tenth grade was when I began to really write, mostly poetry. Millard played piano, and soon the two of us would be writing songs together. Of course, we thought we were going to be huge stars—me writing the lyrics and him singing and playing the piano. He entered several talent shows in high school but never placed higher than second place. The songs were good; his voice wasn't what it needed to be. I didn't care about the voice; I was happy just to hear my words being added to music. It was a great high. I think music in general is a great high. It has a way of marking my life. I can look back to any part of my life and trace the moments—good and bad—to the songs that were popular at that time. And every time I hear that particular song, it triggers the memory and takes me back to the moment. Songs are keepers of life, so to speak. It's like that for me anyway. Ernie thought my writing was really special. He didn't have a clue that a lot of the words were about him.

During my junior year, I let my hair grow. It was usually short, but Mom said as long as I kept it neat and clean, she wouldn't mind if I let it grow longer. I was sitting at the kitchen table doing some homework one afternoon and Dad motioned for me to go with him. I asked where we were going, and he responded, "To the barbershop." I said no. I told him what Mom said, but he didn't hear it. He picked me off the chair and pushed me to the door. I said no again. He grabbed hold of me and pushed me into the car. I waited for him to get in and then I got out. He stepped out of the car and pushed me back in. This went on for a few minutes, and then he hit me in my mouth with his fist. My lip was busted and I started crying. He put me back in the car, and I got out again. He went inside the house and came back out with some handcuffs. He cuffed my hands behind my back, drove me to the barber, set me in the chair, and my hair was cut—with handcuffs on. The barber said, "Well, that's a first!" The barber tried to talk Dad out of it, but his attempt to help me was futile.

Mom came home from work that night and was very sympathetic to me. She apologized for Dad's actions, but it was too late. She told me that I could stay home and not go to school the next day, and I did. I was afraid everyone would laugh at me. When I went to school the day after that, Ernie was one of the first people I saw. He said that it looked good and he really liked it. For me, that made all the difference.

As far as Dad hitting me, it was the second of only two times he ever hit me. He wasn't an affectionate person; he and Uncle John were a lot alike when it came to showing one's feelings, or lack thereof. He rarely told us he loved us; instead, he showed it to us through the things he did. He made sure we had food on the table, clothes on our backs, a house to live in, etc. I believe that he loved us. I really do. If I don't believe that he did, which sometimes I did, then what, pray tell, am I left with?

Chapter 6

Searching for Me

I went to college to get away from home. After that twenty-nine-day hiatus, things weren't any better at home. I was the first one in my senior class to get admission to a university. Mine was to UNC–Chapel Hill. I didn't have a clue what to do with my life, while everyone at school was making plans, picking their careers, so I pretended that I knew what I was doing so I would fit in, and get away from home—again.

Since the first day I arrived in my dorm room, it was party time. No parents, no rules, no curfew—I was on my own. A small circle of friends and I were fixtures at a gay bar named Christopher's in Chapel Hill. We would also drive to Raleigh regularly to indulge at the Capital Corral and the Mousetrap. Disco was at its peak, Donna Summer was the bomb, and we all took advantage. It was dancing, drinking, poppers, cruising, and then repeat as much as possible until closing time. Everyone around was just like myself. It was the first time in my life that people accepted me for being just that—me. I had no car, no income, and I was having the time of my life. I had let my hair grow long (past my shoulders), weighed a whopping 103 pounds, and as was accustomed for the time, arched my eyebrows slightly and took to wearing a little mascara (the bars

44

were dark, and so you had to do what was needed to look good and get noticed—and I was looking good.)

Because I was so slender and had long hair, it was regular for people to approach and ask if I had ever thought of doing drag. I hadn't. People would say, "You should try it, you have the hair, the bone structure, you're slender, you would be great." My friends expressed the same sentiment. One night at Christopher's, the show director approached me and asked if I would be interested in trying out for the show. There are moments in life where things either stay the same or change. Him asking me that question is what changed me. I told him I would do it.

I found myself wearing makeup a little heavier, my eyebrows a little more arched, and in the afternoons, practicing lip-synching to Diana Ross and Barbra Streisand. My roommate at the dorm, weeks earlier, had discovered that his "roomie" was a "homo" and told me to move out. I said, "*I'm* not going anywhere. *You're* the one with the problem, *you* leave." I had the room all to myself for the remainder of the year.

The following week, I auditioned. My nerves were getting the best of me, my knees were buckling, my hands were shaking, and the DJ said, "You're on." I wasn't a good dancer, so I chose a slow song, "Touch Me in the Morning" by Diana Ross. I somehow managed to nail the audition, nerves and all. I was offered a spot in the show—no pay, but would be working for tips. I had no job, no income, I wasn't going to any classes, so tips were better than nothing, and it gave me something to do.

Being a female impersonator or drag queen wasn't something I ever thought about doing. At the time, I really didn't care about drag queens and didn't want to be around them. But I had no direction, and I desperately wanted to be someone, to be accepted, to belong. People were telling me that

I was good, and it seemed to satisfy my need for approval—to be good at something. I always wanted to be the best. If I was the best, then people wouldn't see the worthless, pathetic little boy that Aunt Helen had said I was—the scared little boy she had turned me into. That feeling would follow me through most of my life.

I was set to do the show the following week and would be doing three songs. The next hurdle to get past was clothing. I needed dresses.

A friend of mine let me borrow some money and I went to the mall. I picked out a few dresses and told the salesperson that I was buying them for my sister. The salesperson looked at me as though she knew I was lying. Imagine that, someone lying about buying dresses. How often did that happen? In my next purchases, I would go into the dressing room and try them on—it got to a point where I would fool people. I remember one saleslady opening the fitting room door to ask me how it fit. I said fine, and she said, "Let me know if I can help you with anything else." She didn't even realize I wasn't a woman. The remainder of the week I spent locked in my dorm room rehearsing in front of the mirror. I must have played each song a hundred times, and knew them inside and out, as well as backward.

By Saturday afternoon, the nerves were back in a big way. I had a mixture of emotions—scared, anxious, and excited rolled into one. Needless to say, the cocktail hour started early.

The show was at 10:30 p.m., so I arrived at eight-thirty to get ready. They let us use the back room as a dressing room. There were six entertainers performing—I would perform fourth. By nine-fifteen, I was finished with my hair and makeup and was dressed. It took the other "showgirls" several hours to get ready, and they couldn't believe that I was done so quickly. I didn't have to wear a lot of makeup, which I think bothered them, as they were doing that "whispering" thing.

It was finally ten. I downed two cocktails and waited for my turn. "And now, ladies and gentlemen, we have the pleasure of announcing our newest addition to the show, in her debut, we give you Melanie Brooks." I stood in the doorway, frozen. One of the other girls gave me a push and said, "Show us what you got." I tripped on the carpet—still not used to heels—catching myself with the doorway, but made it to the stage. I grabbed the dead microphone and waited for my music to start. My first song was "Old Souls" from *Phantom of the Paradise*. It was slow, so I thought the mike would add to the realism.

It was over before I knew it. The crowd was on its feet clapping and chanting, "More, more." I got a callback on my first song. I made about sixty bucks in tips, which was really good from what the other girls said. One entertainer only made five dollars in tips for the entire show. The rest of the show for me was a breeze. It just seemed easy after the first song. It wasn't me out there; it was Melanie Brooks—that was how I thought of it, like a character in a play.

After the show, we would mingle around the bar for a while. I felt great walking through that place, with people coming to me and telling me how good I looked, how well I did. Melanie had arrived, and I was feeling good about it.

I went back to the dressing room at closing time to change before going home. While I was trying to pry the falsies off my chest—I used nail adhesive instead of eyelash adhesive (ouch!)—one of the "girls," Erica Van Court, came to me and said, "Girl, you got some people here worried." I asked why and she replied," They're worried 'cause you look so good. You look real." I informed her that I wasn't here to step on anyone's toes.

I just wanted to make some money. During that conversation, we bonded and would later become good friends. Erica and I were the "real" girls in the show, not just guys with a bunch of makeup on, who still looked like guys, as our four colleagues did. Both of us could easily pass as women, without so much effort. We were the "artists."

The next several months came and went, the crowds got larger, and I became everyone's sweetheart—that's how they introduced me: "Everyone's sweetheart, Melanie Brooks." On the inside, I was still very insecure. I wanted to believe what everyone was telling me, but a part of me wouldn't let me believe it. I still felt not good enough. Here I was, wanting to be the best at something I didn't really want to do.

All "female" impersonators have a signature song, one that they are known for, and will always bring in the bucks when it's done. And once you had a signature song, no one else could perform it. It was off-limits. Mine was "Corner of the Sky" by Diana Ross. It was from one of her cutout albums, and it always brought the house down. It was the song that I would do in the upcoming pageant, Miss Gay Chapel Hill, which was a preliminary for Miss Gay North Carolina, and then Miss Gay America.

I want to say that I won the pageant (Erica won), but I was first runner-up, so that ended the pageants for me that year. I did get Miss Congeniality and placed first in talent. I placed second in evening gown and eighth in sportswear. If I had placed better in sportswear, I would have won. I had something to work on.

I spent the next year focusing on Miss North Carolina, and partying, doing the weekly shows in Chapel Hill and Raleigh, and partying, devoting any free time on getting that coveted crown, and partying.

The second semester ended, the dorm was shut down, and I had no place to go. Some friends took pity on me and let me stay with them—seven people in a two-bedroom apartment. I barely got comfortable when the landlord found out and kicked us all out. My only option was to move in with a friend in Raleigh. He was a newcomer in the "biz," and so I kind of became his mentor in exchange for a place to live. This move also meant that I could no longer enter the Miss Chapel Hill pageant. It would now have to be Miss Raleigh.

Before Miss Raleigh, there was a smaller pageant, Miss Summer Fun. I entered and won. I won the talent portion again with my signature song. Two weeks later was Miss Raleigh, and I won.

The following week, my roommate let me know that he was moving to Atlanta, and asked me to go with him. *What do I do now?* Stay and do the Miss North Carolina pageant where I have a good chance at winning, or pack up and move to the "Showplace of the South"—that's how Atlanta was billed. Anyone who is anyone is in Atlanta performing.

We moved to Atlanta in August '79. We moved into an apartment at Twelfth and Piedmont, across from Piedmont Park. I found a job washing dishes at the Gregory's restaurant. The entire staff was gay, so I was at home there. They were well-known for their late-night Bert Burger. While working there, I remember having a chance to meet Dionne Warwick and Morgan Fairchild, who had come in to dine.

For work, my hair was pulled back in a ponytail and I had no makeup on, but it seemed that more men hit on me looking like that than fully dressed out. I would on occasion take a taxi to work when I couldn't find a ride. The taxi drivers would always hit on me, offering me free rides if I would go out with them. I think more straight men asked me out over gay men. Did they think I was a real woman, or were they just curious? I think real girl.

One night at Gregory's, I had gone into the men's bathroom and was standing at the urinal. A gentleman came in, looked at me, and said, "Oh, excuse me, I must be in the wrong one," and he quickly exited. Now, last time I checked, women don't stand at the urinal to relieve themselves, but I took it as a compliment. Management did ask me to start using the women's restroom after the incident. That poor man.

So I washed dishes at night, making the rounds at all the show bars during late night. Three weeks after getting to Atlanta, I had managed to get an audition, and not just any audition. I had gotten an audition at the Sweet Gum Head on Cheshire Bridge Road. This was the gold medal for entertainers, and almost impossible to get your foot in the door. Very cliché, but a friend of a friend had spoken to the show director about me and he agreed to let me "try out." My audition was in four days. I told my roommate about it, and he seemed less than happy for me. He was one of those "boys with a bunch of makeup" people and thought it would be him who would make it in the big city. He almost made me feel bad that I had been given a chance. That feeling lasted about thirty seconds. In four days I would be performing the song of my life in the Showplace of the South. That moment would prove to be a great source of friction in our friendship from that point on.

Audition day. I arrived at the Sweet Gum Head to find out that I was one of four people trying out for one opening in the show: The Diamond Girl Revue. The other three had shown up in full drag. I was wearing a pair of jeans and a T-shirt, carrying my heels to put on when I got on stage. I approached it like a rehearsal. And let me tell you, those other three looked pretty scary in the daylight. I'm guessing about a week's worth of pay was beat into their faces. Something told me they would all do fast songs. When queens aren't good at lip syncing, they tend to do faster songs and dance around so you can't see them flubbing the words. To stand on stage, do a slow song, and not miss a single word or gesture takes talent. It's definitely an art form. I was to go first. I did "Home" from *The Wiz*. It was slow and had a dramatic ending, right up my alley. I would also be using a dead mike. I finished, sat down, and waited for the other three to take their turn. They all did upbeat, dance-type numbers. After all four had finished, we were told that we would be contacted with the decision.

That Saturday night, I was in an after-hours bar, I was half-lit, and the show director from the Sweet Gum Head approached me. He (Tina Devore) said that he liked my audition and would like me to join the show—I about fell over! It just couldn't be that easy—what a validation! He said that I reminded him of himself when he was first starting out.

He said that mandatory rehearsal for the group numbers was on Mondays, and we would be performing on Tuesday and Wednesday nights, with an occasional weekend spot. The weekends were reserved for the headliners—an all-star cast of title holders and crown winners. Rachel Wells (who was the current Miss Gay America), Charlie Brown, Hot Chocolate, Lisa King were some of the big names working there at the time. I was completely beside myself.

So I showed up for the group number rehearsal on Monday. As I said earlier, I couldn't dance very well—choreography was not my friend, so the rehearsal from my end was pretty bad. Individually, I was always prepared and ready, but give me dance steps in a group number and I'm totally lost. If anything was to be my downfall, it would be just that.

Tuesday night came, and I arrived dressed to kill. Hair and makeup couldn't have been better. There were a lot of stares and peering eyes, all coming my way. I was the new girl in the show, and people were trying to figure me out—wondering if they were going to like me or hate me, which in the drag world was really the same thing. Patrons liked you if you were good, and rivals hated you if you were good. If you were good and pretty, the knives were drawn and ready.

My first number was my signature song. It went well, not as much clapping as I thought or expected. The group number for me was a bomb. I messed up the steps. I'm sure the rivals were cheering on the inside. My second song was "Home." Hey, after that group disaster, I needed a good comeback number. Overall, the night was a success, and the first-night jitters were gone. The next couple months came and went without much controversy. The crowds were good, the crowds were bad. I had good nights, I had bad nights. *ETC.* magazine came and took my picture and did a small write-up on me as the newest addition to the cast. *ETC.* was a weekly magazine for the gay community. It had all the latest news—where to go, what to do. Just about everyone I knew read that magazine, and all the bars always had several copies available. It was kinda neat being a minor celebrity and getting in that magazine.

The tension with my roommate was getting worse. It seemed he was angry that I did "Home" for my audition. It was his signature song in North Carolina. We were in Georgia now, and I thought that made a difference. I was in a show and he wasn't—I thought that made a difference. It didn't. I would probably act the same way if the tables were turned. I think part of his anger was really jealousy. I had made it into a cast, and he never would. I think he was also jealous that I was pretty, and he really had to work at it just to come close. Just making an observation.

I was at the bar rehearsing one afternoon. I was early and was the only one there at the time. I was walking around the stage when I noticed someone walk in the front door. This guy walked over to where I was and asked for Tina, the show director. I told him that he wasn't there yet, and he said he would leave a message. He wrote something down on a slip of paper and gave it to me to deliver to Tina. What was unknown to me at the time, that chance meeting, that brief encounter, would alter the course of my life. It would once again change who I was, who I would become, and would cause me to fight the hardest battle any human being should have to face. I would be fighting for my life.

Tina arrived and I gave her the note. We had our rehearsal, and Tina said she wanted to speak to me before I left. After the others filed out, we spoke. He said that he would like for me to start doing some faster, upbeat songs (oh no . . .). He said that a lot of his songs were slow, and doing so many was just too much for the show. It needed to be an even mix. I told him okay (on the outside), but the inside was saying, "No, no, no." *How was I going to fix this?* I went home and spent the rest of the afternoon stressing until I found a solution. I strategically picked songs that were middle of the road—not too fast, not too slow. I wouldn't have to fly around the stage dancing, but instead would be able to walk around with a little bit of step in my walk. A song like "Just One Look" by Linda Ronstadt could work. It was worth a try.

I did the song Tuesday night, and it worked pretty well, so I chose a few more songs along that line to work on. During the Wednesday show, I noticed that guy from rehearsal in the audience. I assumed he had come to see Tina. During the break between shows, Tina went out and sat with him briefly. I went to the bar to fetch a cocktail. That's what we in the biz called it, "fetching a cocktail." I turned to head back to the dressing room, and there he was, standing behind me.

"You did really great tonight. I've been around a lot of female impersonators, and you are one of the best I've seen."

I said thank you.

"My name is Jason."

"Melanie Brooks."

"I know."

"I guess you would."

It was pretty stupid telling him who I was; after all, they announce us by our stage name before each of the songs we perform. I walked away feeling a little embarrassed. I looked back in his direction as I was walking, and he had a look on his face, a smile, as if he knew I would turn around and look at him. I gave a quick smile, like I'd been caught, and continued to the dressing room.

I noticed that he was starting to come to every show and always tried to talk to me. I always kept it polite, and brief. I finally asked Tina who he was, and she replied he was just a friend. As coincidence would have it, this was the night he asked me out. Well, someone kick me in the ass, as I said yes.

We went out for the next few weeks and started getting to know each other. I learned that he had two children, a girl and a boy, who was staying with his father in Alabama until he could get them here. He was a mechanic, working in a gay-owned garage on Peachtree Street. He was somewhat private about most of his personal life, but I did find out that he had been adopted. He had gotten his own apartment when he was sixteen and, by the time I met him, had gone through nineteen cars. His mother had died when he was young and used that against his father to get whatever he wanted. It seemed that his mother had gotten quite sick, and his father didn't take her to the hospital and she died. His father didn't realize how sick she really was. Jason grew up in New York, with Jewish parents who were both guidance counselors for the New York school system. He said one of his classmates in high school was Cass Elliott, from the Mamas & the Papas. I learned that he had been in trouble with the law numerous times, but nothing serious according to him. Something I found odd after a couple of weeks was that every time I tried to be intimate with him, he backed away. Another odd thing was that he went to sleep fully clothed. I chalked it up to him being shy, or not being out of the closet very long. After three weeks, which is a long time in gay life, I began pressing a little harder for some answers. He said the lack of intimacy was "wanting to be sure it was right" and sleeping fully clothed was just more of the same. I let him know that I felt people should be intimate as part of the process of getting to know one another and left it at that. After the show that night, we came home and got ready for bed.

Chapter 7

Hell Is Back

I came out of the bathroom, and he was already in bed, this time with his clothes off. I crawled into bed and reached over to touch him. As I touched him, I got this uneasy feeling inside me. He didn't feel right. Strange thing to say, but he didn't. He had no body hair whatsoever. My hand was on his waist, and I let it wander down his hip (I started feeling rather uncomfortable) and on to his leg. Something just wasn't right. My hand moved up from the leg over to the crotch area. My God, there was nothing there! Well, there was something there, but it wasn't anything a man has! Jason was a woman!

As I jumped out of bed, I shouted, "What in the *hell* is going on?"

After he dressed, Jason started explaining the whole story to me. He had started reconstructive surgery, but hadn't completed it as of yet. He said the surgery would be finished in the next couple years. (I use "he" when referring to Jason. but now that you know, I am more comfortable using "they" or "them" when referring to them, instead of "he" or "she." Let me say here that I have never thought of Jason, after the truth was out, as a man; I have never thought of Jason as a woman. For the sake of this book and fluidity, I will use "he.")

I was really at a loss for words and was furiously hoping my brain would shed some light, give me some answers, but it just wasn't coming. I sat there with a blank face through most of his explanation. How could I have been so stupid not to have figured it out? The signs were there, slapping me in the face, and I didn't see it. The wide hips, no face hair or even stubble, the small feet, no Adam's apple—I am such an idiot.

It's raining outside. In the middle of all this mess, my mind is telling me it's raining outside. I hope it's not raining tomorrow, as I have a show to do. Okay, brain, focus.

The only thing I could come up with to deal with this "situation" was, "Jason, I want to see other people." Now, he looked at me as if I had just committed a cardinal sin. He was truly shocked at what I just said. My follow-up was a little better: "I need some time to take all this in and sort it out, so I would like you to leave, tonight." Jason gathered his things and made way to the door. He was crying as he left, out into the pouring rain. It was really a sad picture to watch him walk down the street and out of sight. I went back to my room and sat there, trying to make sense with my brain. After about thirty minutes, and almost asleep, the doorbell rang. I got up and went to the door. I opened it, and there he was, standing all drenched, still crying. Jason asked me to please give him a chance, as he was all alone and only wanted someone in this world to care about him. I spent most of my life feeling alone and uncared for, so the being alone part really got to me. Other than the drag, my life was a vacant parking lot of monotony, a broken record playing over and over again. I gave in. I said yes. This would have been my first "out," the first chance to rid my life of the headache, and I unknowingly threw it away. We were now, officially, a couple.

I asked Jason, if he wanted to be a man, why then did he want to be with me? It seemed that he would want to be with a woman. Jason said that he couldn't help how he felt; he enjoyed being around me, and that's all he knew. I told him that I wasn't in love with him, and he said sooner or later I would be, once I knew him better.

Within a few weeks of the epiphany, Jason had quit the job at the garage. He said the people in charge didn't like him and was giving him a hard time. I was still working at Gregory's and the Sweet Gum Head, barely scraping by, but Jason always seemed to have money (where he got it from, I don't know). He took a job at the service station by the apartment, and within two weeks had quit—same excuse as the last job. As time went by, Jason started showing up more and more at my work. He said it was just to check in, but the truth was he was showing up unannounced to see if he could catch me talking to someone—a guy. Jason was turning out to have quite a jealous streak. If I happened to be talking to a co-worker who was male, Jason would get into their face, accusing them of some impropriety. It was extremely embarrassing, even more so when I'd be talking to my bosses. The manager eventually asked Jason to stop coming around when I was working, but it didn't deter him. My manager finally called me in his office and, although very happy with my employment, was going to let me go.

Jason seemed happy that I was home during the day now, but I wasn't. I got a job at another restaurant working in the kitchen. When I told Jason, he got really angry. It seemed he liked me underfoot, where he could keep an eye on me better. Within a week, Jason was calling my job several times a day. When my boss told him I was busy, he would show up, making a scene. This was all very frustrating, and I was very apologetic to my boss, but after a dozen times of this, enough was enough. I was fired. Again, Jason seemed happy.

Jason was at every show I did at the Sweet Gum Head. It got to the point where, after I finished a number, I had to sit with him. During the breaks, if a gentleman would compliment me or offer to buy me a drink, Jason would go nuts. I would try to explain the innocence of the whole thing to him, but he wasn't hearing it. "You want him, don't you?" "You want to sleep with him," "I saw you looking at him," were typical of the things Jason would throw at me. It was around this point in time when Jason started throwing more than words at me. He would push me, then apologize. He would hit me, then apologize. Jason had gotten very possessive and dominating in a very short time. I was never without him for very long when he would just show up out of the blue. He had started threatening me with violence worse than I had already received from him if I left. Jason threatened to kill himself and take me with him. Before I knew it, I was in the thick of it and didn't know how to get out. I really thought if I stuck it out, he would change—calm down. I thought he would eventually see that I wasn't doing anything wrong. The fights were getting to be a daily thing, and my roommate had spoken to me about putting an end to it. He said that either Jason went, or we both went. I told him that I would figure it out.

I was slowly being isolated from all my friends. I couldn't go and hang out with them without Jason showing up making a scene. They were getting tired of dealing with the mess and disappeared one by one. The only friends we had were Jason's friends, or friends we met together. Through it all, I lost a lot of great friends. Even a lot of the female impersonators were starting to keep their distance to avoid the headache Jason would cause.

I was in my bedroom getting ready for a show and heard voices in the living room. I came out to see who it was and found

Jason and a few of his friends lighting up a joint. These people I hadn't met before. Jason introduced them as Tricia, Nikki, and Mark. One look at Mark and it was all over. I fell in love that day. I didn't know it at the time, but I was head over heels—literally. I was so shy that I couldn't bring myself to speak to him. The words just wouldn't come out. I felt like he could see right through me. I did the only thing I knew to do—I went back into the bedroom. How was this going to turn out, I wondered, me, being smitten with Jason's best friend.

Mark had started coming around a lot more, always with Jason in tow. Mark could put a smile on my face like no other could. I was always so embarrassed when Jason would fight with me while Mark was around. Mark ran interference as much as he could. Mark always seemed to have this "It's going to be okay" look in his eyes during Jason's bouts with anger. I just knew from Mark's face, he understood it wasn't my fault. During those unbearable moments of intimacy with Jason, I would pretend it was Mark. Maybe it was wishful thinking on my part, but I really felt like Mark had the same feelings for me as I did for him. I would always catch him looking at me, and he'd blush every time I caught him. After a while, he stopped blushing and would just smile. Yeah, I think he felt the same way. He was so damned handsome.

I was losing a lot of sleep, with doing the shows and hanging out afterward, barhopping 'til seven in the morning, arguing with Jason the rest of the time. Every now and then, I would get a moment or two alone with Mark, and I really loved those few moments. Jason recommended that I take a hit of speed before a show to liven me up and balance out the loss of sleep. That night at the bar, Jason gave me a "speckled bird." Thirty minutes later, I was speeding my ass off. I felt great, the life of the party.

I couldn't believe that a little pill could make you feel so good. I was given a pill every night before a show. After a few weeks, I had started taking them when I woke up. Within a month, I was climbing the walls without them. When I didn't have one, I felt like I hadn't slept in a year. I could tell that my performances were beginning to suffer and blamed it on Jason's confrontational attitude. There really wasn't a time when we weren't arguing— Jason would argue and I would say and do what he wanted just to put an end to it.

Most of the arguing stemmed from a lack of intimacy. Jason wanted it; I didn't want to give it. His response to the situation was "forcing" me to do it. He would mentally and physically tear me down until I gave in. When I didn't give in soon enough, he would hold me down and take it. When it was over, I could breathe easier for a few days, until he wanted it again. Jason said that my performance suffering wasn't because of him. He said that it was me, and I needed to be more "real"-looking if I wanted to get anywhere. He said I should start hormone therapy, which would enhance my features and make me look even more feminine than I already did. Hormone therapy would give me the extra edge that was needed to move ahead. Sounds crazy, but Jason was almost making sense. Where had I gone? Little pieces of myself were falling away as time went by. How much more time would go by before I was no longer recognizable to myself? What Jason was saying—what Jason wanted me to do—was not who I was.

When we got home that evening, after Jason went to sleep, I went outside on the back porch to get some alone time. This evening would find me sober and drug-free, which was rare. It was beginning to rain, which felt very soothing as it fell on my skin. I had a cigarette lit and was taking a moment to reflect—

one of those brief moments when you just want to slow down and breathe. "What are you going to do?" is the one question I remember asking myself. I asked it over and over again. I just can't do this anymore, but how do I get out? Where can I go? Jason will find me. I know this because Jason drilled it into my brain with his fist every other day. I didn't get any answers that night, but knew that a change was coming. I had to get Myles back.

Jason was MIA again. I wasn't allowed to go anywhere without him, but he said that he was free to do whatever he wanted (according to him). A friend stopped by to say hi and play catch-up before going to work. His name was Michael and was a hairdresser by trade. After a few minutes of chatting, I asked him if he had his scissors with him. He said yes, and I asked him to bring them in. He retrieved them from the car and returned to the living room. I said, "Cut it, cut it all off." His eyes got big and his mouth dropped about three feet.

"Are you sure?"

"Yes."

"Girl, you're gonna break some faces!"

I sat down in the chair, and the scissors began the transformation. I could see the hair falling all around me, and it was quite therapeutic in a sense. It felt like all the layers were peeling away with each clip. It was all washing away. Once Michael had finished, he covered my eyes and walked me to the bathroom, putting me in front of the mirror. He counted down 3, 2, 1, and moved his hands. I couldn't believe it! It was really gone! Standing in front of me in the mirror was Myles. The boy was back, with arched eyebrows. It was done and I felt better. I felt good about making a decision and following through with it, but panic was starting to settle in. Jason wasn't going to be happy. I feared the mother of all fights coming my way. I looked at it this way: if Jason wanted a woman, then maybe seeing me as a man would force him to realize the truth and leave.

I took the eyebrow pencil and tried to fill in the area that was missing. It would take some practice, but it was passable. I would also need to buy some men's clothes as money allowed. Most of my wardrobe was of the female persuasion. I had one pair of jeans and a few T-shirts, and that was it.

My roommate came home from work and was startled when he saw me. There was a second or two there when he actually didn't know who I was. Once the initial shock wore off, he said I looked like a real boy, which means he liked it. He was also happy that I had decided to stop the drag. I'm sure there was a moment in there when he thought he had a chance to take my spot in the show—wouldn't happen.

Jason walked in, looked at me, immediately went to the bedroom, and shut—no, slammed—the door. When the sounds of things breaking started, my roommate and I both flew out the front door. We went to a neighborhood bar for a while to give Jason a chance to cool down. While I was there, this really good-looking guy approached and started a conversation. He said that he had seen me around several times and wanted to ask me out, but was told by other people to stay away from me (because of Jason). It wasn't long before Jason showed up. I braced for the worst. He walked up to me and said, "I don't care what you look like. I fell in love with you for the person you are, not what you look like." Not quite the response I was looking for, yet another chance to get free gone to the wayside. I think Jason wanted to be with someone so bad, and wanted to be loved so desperately, that, at all cost, he would hold on to any glimmer of a chance of having it. Jason was intelligent enough to know that I didn't love him. I really believe he thought he could make me.

We got home that night, and any understanding Jason had about the haircut, about quitting drag, went up in smoke. I was pushed around, choked, bitten, punched, the usual stuff. This go-round would leave me with a broken rib. The following morning, my roommate told me that he wanted Jason and me to move out.

As luck would have it, and I didn't have much of it, a friend of mine from Gregory's restaurant was moving in with his other half and said we could take over his apartment. The apartment building was located on the corner of Peachtree Street and Ponce DeLeon, across from the Fox Theatre. It gave us a month to find jobs and hopefully get on our feet.

We spent the next few days moving in and job hunting. I landed a job on week 2, but on the morning I was to start, Jason said he didn't want me to go. He said that he wanted us to both work together somewhere. How often does that happen? What are the chances that we would get hired at the same place? After some arguing, I gave in, not wanting it to escalate into something physical. I always knew Jason's breaking point. I would often take it to the limit, stopping just short of that point. When we argued, I would hold out a little longer each time, thinking I was gaining some kind of edge. Bottom line was that Jason would always win—one way or the other. The days and months ahead didn't look promising.

The next few jobs I landed went the same way as the first one. When the end of the month came around, we didn't have the money to pay for rent. We were going to have to move, again. This time around, Jason called his father and asked for money. His dad drove to Atlanta from Gadsden, Alabama, to bring him the badly needed funds.

Jason had told his father that he wanted to settle down and get straightened out so he could get his children back. His father seemed to like the idea of Jason finally getting on the right path. We found an apartment across from Ansley Mall on Monroe Drive. Once again I was out hunting a job. I managed to get hired at Morrison's Cafeteria in Ansley Mall. When I told Jason that I found a job, he went across the street and applied at the same place. He got hired.

Jason worked in the storeroom while I worked as the cashier. A month or so went by and we both still had our jobs. The bills were getting paid most of the time—Jason still found reasons to go out and buy drugs—Acid was his drug of choice. It was around this time when Jason decided we had to have tattoos. He wanted us to put each other's name on our upper arm. Jason got his way— always—and I ended up with a red heart on my arm with his name in the middle. I remember the tattoo artist asking me my name, and I had to say Jason. Who puts their own name on their arm anyway? I'm sure that tattoo artist knew the real deal. I would eventually end up with three tattoos on my arm.

Jason spoke to his father again about getting the kids. I tried to speak with him about the situation. We clearly were not ready to take on kids. We had no money put away, we were fighting daily, and we had no car. We also were dealing with a more than occasional drug use.

Jason wouldn't have any part of listening. He wanted his kids, and that was that. He conned his father into buying a car for us, and that completed the need list in his eyes.

The following week, Morris brought Ginger and Daniel to the apartment to move in. They had never met me before, but took to me quite easily. Ginger, seven, was very outgoing while Daniel, two, was very shy and quiet. We spent the weekend getting to know each other and helping them adjust to the new living arrangement. On Monday, Jason went and got Ginger registered for school. As Daniel wasn't old enough to start, Morris agreed to temporarily hire a housekeeper to watch him during the day so we could work. So that's the way it went for a while. We played house and acted like a normal family when we were anything but normal. We even got a kitten and puppy to complete the pretty little picture.

The kids being with us didn't stop any of the fighting. I tried my best to keep everything smooth and as uncomplicated as possible, but Jason never seemed to care what was going on or who was around when he got into one of his moods. He wasn't happy and everyone had to suffer.

One particular day, I came home to Jason telling me he wanted to talk. The next thing out of his mouth was, "I'm pregnant." I was floored. First, I didn't know Jason could get pregnant. I thought he had that taken care of medically. I mean, if you want to be a man, why would you want to keep those female parts? Second, what were we going to do now? Jason said he was going to get an abortion. I said no. I always wanted to be a father. There was a driving force inside me ever since my teens—to be a dad. I always pictured myself being a father someday and played it all out in my head. I felt I would be a good father, not repeating any of the things that had made my life so sad. My kids would know that they were loved. I knew Jason had no business being a parent. I never heard him tell the kids that he loved them. I don't remember him ever showing them any affection. I figured I would be enough of a parent for the both of us.

Jason said we couldn't afford another child. "You should have thought about that when you were making me get on top of you." Oops, I shouldn't have said that. Jason went into his rage and beat the crap out of me. He did this with the kids in the apartment. I was getting my ass kicked, and all I could think of was the kids. After the fight, I asked Jason to please not get an abortion, but he wouldn't give me a promise. The next few days were very quiet around the home front. There was this unspoken conversation hanging in the air. Both of us knew what the other wanted and felt; it was written on our faces. I really wanted this baby, heart and soul I wanted it, and my life force desperately needed it. I knew I would be a great father and wanted a chance to prove it. Days had passed with no decision being made, or so I thought. I came home from work to find Jason in the bathroom, hemorrhaging badly. There was newspaper spread all over the bathroom floor covered with blood. Jason said that he had gotten an abortion and that he wasn't clotting like he was supposed to. All I could do was slam the bathroom door and walk away. I hoped he would bleed to death. What had I done in my life that would warrant so much pain? As I walked away from the bathroom, I felt pieces of myself falling away from my body, like candle wax dripping away from the candle, disappearing into the air.

The next morning, I called Jason's father and told him about all the fighting and the abortion. I told him the kids didn't need to be here, enduring all this mess. He agreed. Within a few days, he showed up at the apartment to pick up the kids. When he told Jason that I called him, he jumped up from his chair, throwing me against the wall. He grabbed my throat with both hands, choking me until I blacked out. I awoke to Jason hitting me repeatedly. I could hear Morris in the background telling Jason to stop. He wouldn't let up. I could feel the blood running down my face. Jason finally stopped when Morris threatened to call the police. Morris and the kids left. With a bloodied face, I asked Jason why he didn't just let me leave. He said, "Because I love you."

Picture Section

Marie, my birth mother, circa 1955

Aunt Helen, taken just before she passed

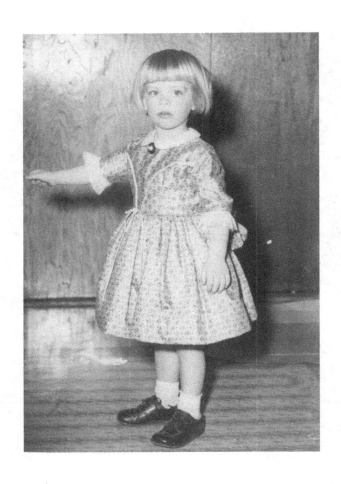

Jason as a child, when he was known as Joyce

Childhood photo of Jason, age 7 or 8

Me and my twin, May 1959, 1 year old

Mike and I, 1 year old

Taken at the house in Milan, 1964, we were 6

Melanie Brooks, circa 1978

Senior graduation photo, 1977

Melanie Brooks, circa 1979

Miss Gay Raleigh pageant, 1979 (my own hair)

Jason and Taron, May 2000
(Jason shot himself 2 weeks later)

Chapter 8

As Good as it Gets?

It was around this time when I became a self-induced OCD. I thought if I could stay busy cleaning, then I wouldn't have to spend any time with Jason. I threw myself into it completely. I cleaned every nook and cranny, over and over again. Whenever Jason would complain he wasn't getting enough attention, I would suggest that he help me clean, to get it done faster. He wouldn't have it—men don't do housework. For the most part, it worked. I cleaned myself right into a disorder! Friends would come over, and I would take their glasses before they were done drinking and wash it, bring them a new drink, and then do it all over again. I would be dusting around them the whole time I was talking with them. I had the cleanest apartment in the Southeast! There were still those times when Jason won out over the cleaning. I wish I could tell you how badly I hated it. I always tried to be under the influence of something, anything, to lessen the nausea. I would pretend he was someone else I was having sex with. I would tell myself that I liked it, that I wanted to do it. The reality of it all always kept me from drifting away for very long. Several months had passed when Jason told me he was pregnant again. Not wanting a repeat of the first, I let him know again that I really wanted this baby. I spoke about all the positives, how this would give him a chance at a fresh start, correcting the mistakes of the past. I even lied and said that I thought he would be a good parent. I would talk about the baby coming every day with Jason, hoping he was on board with seeing it through. I had put some money away—a little here, a little there—in an envelope I hid under the carpet of the bedroom. I knew if Jason was aware of the money, it would have been gone. By the time the baby gets here, there should be enough saved to leave. The baby and I could get away—leave, to a new life.

Jason didn't let up on his drinking or drug use. He was also taking male hormones. I would voice my concern about the baby, but Jason said everything would be fine—he had it under control. It was about six weeks later when he told me. He had gotten another abortion. Are there any words? No, there's not. Other than Aunt Helen, I don't think I've hated someone more. Jason had taken away a piece of my soul, and that is something you can't ever get back. I still had the money put away. A little longer and I could leave, ridding myself of this dark abyss of a person. I spoke to Jason only when it was absolutely necessary. The cleaning became more extreme, staying up 'til the wee hours—dusting, mopping, waxing, and polishing. Jason would holler at me from the bedroom to come to bed, but I ignored him. So what if he hit me. I took a reflection of my life and soon after came to the conclusion that the 50/50 chance I had of losing my life didn't seem all that bad. I think anyone who has gone through a constant beat down gets to a point when they give up—throw in the towel. When you know on a daily basis that maybe today is the day you will lose your life, you kind of get numb to the whole thing. My life was a mess—had been for most of it. So what if he hit me. I decided from this moment on I would give back whatever he threw at me, whatever came my way.

Jason came to the epiphany that all our problems were a result of where we lived—in the city. His newest idea was to move out of the city into the suburbs. With the exception of losing my job again, I didn't care. Moving out of the city to fix the problem was like using gas to put out a fire. I knew it wasn't going to solve anything.

He spoke to his father about his moment of brilliance, and Morris once again thought it was a good idea, so we moved. This time around, the move took us to Mableton, to a double-wide at the end of a dead-end road. Morris put up the money for the down payment, with the understanding Jason would pay it back. Good luck with that.

Jason allowed me to use the car to go and apply for some jobs. I was surprised he didn't come along, but it was a welcome break. Within a week, I had landed an interview at a county animal shelter. I was really hoping I would get the job—I've always loved animals, and helping those who couldn't speak appealed to me. The phone call came two days later that I had gotten the job. The pay was really good, and it had good benefits. This was definitely a step up for me. More money meant that I could put a bit more into my stash under the carpet. It turned out my new supervisor was a lesbian. We became friends rather quickly, and she became my confidant. It was really good to have someone I could bare all with. I guess I must have over glorified my job, as Jason decided to go and apply. I dreaded the idea of him getting the job and really hoped that he wouldn't. The "forces that be" must have been looking down on me—he didn't get the job. When they ran his name through for the background check, his photo and female name came up. They thought they had put two and two together and turned him down for employment. I was breathing a little easier. I wanted him to find a job, just not one with me. Jason, for some reason, thought it was my fault he didn't get the job. He accused me of talking to management, asking them not to hire him. Right in the middle of defending myself to him, out of nowhere, Jason hit me with a closed fist in the face. He broke my glasses, cutting my eye pretty badly. I found myself once again bleeding at the hand of Jason. Guess he didn't learn that rule about not hitting someone with glasses on. I told the people at work that I tripped getting out of bed. It was about here, for the next year or so, when his temper and behavior would really begin to spiral out of control.

Jason allowed me to drive the car to work, but was angry about it at the same time. He couldn't show up unannounced without a vehicle. He made up for it with constant phone calls. My manager was aware of Jason's personality, which made it a little less stressful to deal with. It came to a point when they asked him to stop calling and told him they wouldn't page the calls through. My bosses were very pleased with my work performance and didn't let Jason's antics reflect directly on me. I felt very welcome at my new job. I began working some overtime, putting me at home less—which I liked. Work had become a sanctuary from the misery I left at my front door every morning and night. I dreaded having to clock out for the day and making that drive home. I never knew which Jason I was going to be greeted by, and the odds were not in my favor very often. I couldn't be late getting home, ever. Seriously, I had better not get stuck in traffic or make any stops en route to home, or there would be hell to pay. He knew I got home at 4:45 p.m. If I got home at 4:50

p.m., he would accuse me of stopping to meet with someone. If I didn't get home precisely on time, I was cheating. He would make me remove my clothes so he could inspect me for signs of having sex with a man. If I put up any kind of fight, he would rip and tear them off of me.

Sometimes, all I could do was laugh at him, which really pissed him off. On one of those occasions, he rammed his finger inside me, saying, "Is that what you want? Is that how you like it?" This went on for several minutes. The pain drove me to tears, which seemed to satisfy him on some level. I was constantly being punished for Jason not being a man. I hated days when I got stuck in traffic. .

It was August 1981. I was leaving work for the day. I got in the car and it wouldn't crank. After several attempts at trying to get it started, I threw in the towel and caught a ride with a co-worker. When we pulled up in front of the house, Jason was standing at the front door—this wasn't going to go well. When Jason saw that the person giving me a ride was a guy, I could tell he had snapped. He threw open the door and started toward the car. I thanked my ride and hurried out of the car so he could get on his way before Jason started anything with him. "Who in the hell was that, one of your boyfriends? So that's why you come home late . . . you're sleeping with him, aren't you!"

I tried to tell Jason what happened, but his mind was made up. He said, "I got something to fix this little party. Yeah, I'm gonna fix this real good." He turned and went inside the house. What does that mean? What's going on? Do I go in the house? Do I need to run? Something about the scene felt different. I opted to go in the house and meet whatever head-on. As I got inside and headed toward the bedroom, I saw the gun in his hand. I turned and ran out the door into the wooded area behind the house. Did he see me? Where in the hell did the gun come from? I planted myself behind the biggest tree I could find, where I could still see the house. Jason stepped out, and I saw him walking around looking for me. When he got frustrated at not finding me, he just started shooting at random into the woods, hoping to hit me with one of the bullets. Somehow I needed to get to a phone. I waited about forty-five minutes for Jason to go back inside and then cut through the woods to the convenient store about a half mile from home. The pasture I had to cross was really muddy from the rain earlier in the day. My boots kept sinking in the muck that at times was almost to the top of my boot. All the way to the store, I kept asking myself, "Is this it? Is this really as good as my life is ever gonna get?" I mean, really . . .

I got to a phone and called my manager. She came and picked me up, and I asked her to come back to the house with me to make sure it was safe. She was aware of my situation and versed in Jason's personality; she was hesitant, but agreed. We got back to the house, and Jason was sitting in front of the TV like nothing had happened. My manager verified my story and asked Jason to give her the gun. Surprisingly, he gave it to her. I think he realized that I was telling the truth about my ride home. He promised my boss that nothing else would happen that evening, and it didn't. I did sleep with one eye open.

The next few months came and went without much incident. There were still the arguments, mostly about intimacy, but not anything big or blown out. I kinda figured Jason was trying to give me the benefit of the doubt after the gun incident. Jason attempted to apply for work (so he said)—still calling me several times a day to make sure I was at work. I think, by now, everyone at work knew the story about Jason. I would get to work in the morning and walk into the break room to clock in. As I walked in the room, I felt like I had just interrupted something. Everyone would stop talking and look at me. It was a very uneasy feeling to know that I was the subject of their conversation; I felt violated in a way. I didn't bother anyone and didn't want anyone to bother me; I just came in and did my job. I was expecting them to do the same.

Chapter 9

My Baby

I'll never forget it. It was November 26, 1981, when I found out. It was Thanksgiving evening, and Jason wanted us to drive into Atlanta to see a show at the Sweet Gum Head. He called Mark (yeah), and he met us there. I always like being around Mark. He had a good sense of humor and had a free, boyish charm about him. He was quite striking to look at. He always made me smile when he was around. Jason always thought of Mark as "his" friend, not mine.

Jason had stepped outside to smoke a cigarette. Mark turned to me and said, "Look, Myles, Jason is not the person you need to be with. He is not going to make you happy. You need to be with a man—a real man, someone who can give you what you want and need. That someone is me. I want to give that to you."

Well, isn't that a fine pickle. Mark was someone who I was really comfortable with. And I had thought about it almost daily since becoming friends. It's one of those things when you're around someone, and you know that you both know it, and feel the connection. We had that. Jason came back to the table before I could respond to Mark. We spent the rest of the night stealing glances at each other, wondering what if. Thinking about Mark, as always, was a very pleasant diversion.

One of Mark's best friends was this blond named Billy. They were together a lot, running around to all the bars, drinking and dancing 'til the wee hours. Anyway, Billy had another friend that would hang around with them a lot on these barhopping nights. Billy's friend was this really tall, lanky black guy who was very boisterous and "in your face." This guy was an up-and-coming female impersonator by the name of RuPaul. Just thought I'd do some name-dropping . . .

It's still very clear in my head. We got home that night, and Jason said, "I'm pregnant again."

"God damn it! Why do you keep letting this happen! I can't take it, not another abortion. I can't go through that again! Do you hear me? We are going to have this baby, or I am leaving! I mean it! I will leave! No matter what you do to me—shoot me, stab me, run me over, I will still leave!"

Jason looked surprised. I think he knew I was serious about leaving this time—it was "put up or shut up" time, and I was ready to go the distance for this baby. Jason said if I swore I wouldn't leave, then he would not get an abortion. I swore it a hundred times to him that night. There was one little glitch in all of this—Mark.

Within a few days of getting together, Mark had started calling me at work. When I heard his voice on the other end of the phone, it made me smile. My boss commented once, after seeing me smiling on the phone, I couldn't be talking to Jason or I wouldn't be smiling. Mark had this way of allowing me to drift away from everything negative, making me want that better life, making me want to find that light in the storm. Mark was proof that things could be better in life—good things really are out there. He always seemed to know my moods and knew exactly what to say to make my sometimes hectic day better. On this phone call, he spoke about wanting to get together for some alone time, but that would prove to be a very difficult task to accomplish. Besides, he was now aware of the baby and the two previous abortions. Both of us didn't want to do anything that would compromise the baby's safe arrival. Life just wasn't going to make this easy. There had better be one hell of a prize at the end of all this.

Jason said he wanted to get a house, a real house, for the baby. He again spoke to his father, telling him the situation, our intentions to keep the baby, and wanting to get a house instead of living in a mobile home. He agreed. Jason decided we needed to be farther away from the city than we already were. West is where he wanted to go, so there we were, driving up Interstate 20 to Douglasville. He found a house that he liked, which was about twenty miles from work. Being that far away, I would have to get up a lot earlier to get to work on time—I was already getting up at 5:30 a.m. to be at work by seven. I would make the additional sacrifice if it meant getting into a house.

Within two weeks, Morris had closed on the house, using the mobile home as the down payment. He had the house put in his name—I guess he knew Jason better than I thought he did. He was actually very aware of the monster he had helped create in Jason. I believe he was very regretful of that fact. And I also believe that he hoped each monetary act of kindness would be the end of it. The weariness in his face told of a man ready for some peace and quiet.

Life in Douglasville was quiet. The newly built subdivision we moved into was near empty. Even though it wasn't, the city itself seemed very rural. It had a very "country" feel to it—definitely not the place for a wannabe transsexual to be having a baby. We would really have to be careful not to let anyone find out.

We wouldn't have the money to pay for the hospital or delivery when the time came, so Jason drove into Atlanta to apply for help through the Medicaid office instead of applying in Douglasville. He got approved, and arrangements were made with Crawford Long Hospital for the birth. They gave him an alias so no one would find out about our strange but true story. This was a very happy time for me as I realized that Jason was past the first trimester and couldn't get an abortion. I was actually, in a few short months, going to be a father, a daddy, a man with responsibility. I loved saying that word—father.

Mark continued to call me at work and still came over to visit often—always when Jason was there. Things were always calmer around the house when Mark was there. Jason liked him coming by as much as I did. The only thing that bothered me was Jason would drink beer or alcohol when Mark came over. He didn't drink to excess, but for me, the amount was still too much. I never saw them, but I'm sure they had smoked a few joints during Mark's visits. I spoke to both of them about being careful, for the baby's sake. They halfway acknowledged. I would have to keep a closer eye on them.

We got through Christmas without any incident, and December turned into January. Jason went in for his regular visit with the baby's doctor in the middle of the month. I had started going with him to the appointments initially, but all the people in the waiting room would stare us down. The room was full of pregnant women. They would call Jason's name, and you could see it on their faces, trying to figure out what the deal was. Two guys walk in, one gets called to the back. Where's the mother? It was very hard for me to deal with, so after the first two visits, I just told Jason that I couldn't get off work. When I got home from work on this scheduled visit, Jason said they did the ultrasound, and it was a boy. I was hoping for a little girl. Don't get me wrong, I'd have been happy either way, as long as a healthy baby made it into this world. My preference, if I was allowed to choose, would have been for a girl. I had always pictured myself being a father to a little girl, playing it all out in my head. She was going to grow up to be Miss America. No problem, though, just had to pick out a boy's name now. After a few weeks, we had decided on Aaron Mathew. I really liked the sound of it. It was a good, strong name. Aaron's due date was May 30.

Word had gotten out at work about me becoming a father. It wasn't a surprise to me that everyone was in shock and in disbelief. I was definitely the talk of that place for a while! The little sissy boy was going to be a dad. Most of my fellow employees thought it was a made-up story. I would have to have slept with a woman! Myles slept with a woman? What did Jason think about that? It was all pretty humorous around there for some time. What was unexpected was the way I was treated after they found out. People who didn't give me the time of day before were now making conversation with me. People were getting friendlier toward me, like I was less gay or no longer gay. How backward is that? Even though they had decided to throw a few words my way, it in no way meant they were my friends. As some of them would later prove, they were as empty as their words, as fake as their smiles— they were plastic. Anyway, I wasn't there for the people; I was there to take care of the animals. The people were just casualties of the job that were dealt with as needed.

On Jason's next appointment, the doctor put him on a strict diet. His latest tests showed that he was mildly diabetic. The doctor said it was due to the pregnancy. Jason wasn't happy about the dietary changes. A lot of the stuff he liked was not on the list. I think the pregnancy was really wearing on his mental state. It was very draining on him walking around as a man, with a baby in his stomach. It was his choice not to get the hysterectomy, for whatever reason. I had very little sympathy for his situation. Jason had always said the reason he didn't finish the surgery was due to a lack of money, but that was a lie. It had been proven to me over and over again that Morris would have paid for it if Jason had asked. Morris, to my knowledge, had never told Jason no his entire life. So if money wasn't the real issue, then what was? That is a question that Jason never gave me an honest answer to. My speculation is that Jason wasn't a true transsexual. Someone who is in the wrong body would have done whatever they could to fix the problem as quickly as humanly possible. They would feel incomplete until they did. They certainly wouldn't be getting pregnant over and over again. Jason was nothing like that. I think he wanted to look like a man, act like a man, and that's where it ended. I think Jason allowed himself to get too swept up with the "act" and was in need of some serious therapy. His mind was battling, but it was nothing that a sex change would ever be able to fix. I was there, in the thick of it, living it every day, and that is my conclusion on Jason.

It had now been close to three years since I had touched another man. My libido was in overdrive. Somehow, some way, I need to find a way to make it happen. It was beginning to interfere with my daily life. I would shake hands with a man, or brush past one, and I could feel my body temperature start shooting up. The tension was giving me headaches, and the fantasies were becoming more frequent and more consuming. I was struggling in a big way. I had never stepped out on anyone I was in a relationship with. I wouldn't classify what Jason and I had as a relationship, but we were together, thus my dilemma. Mentally, I had already cheated every time I spoke to or saw Mark. Do I forego what I feel strongly about—monogamy—or do I suffer it out, knowing that I would be free at some point to ease the tension, hopefully sooner than later? We'll see.

It was getting close to the due date. With the exception of the doctor visits, Jason had taken to not leaving the house at all. He thought it was obvious that he was pregnant, but most people who didn't know wouldn't have guessed. It was hard for me to tell just by looking at him. He was heavier, but didn't have that obvious "giant bubble" look attached at the stomach. Anyway, staying home was right up his alley. Being pregnant meant he had an excuse for not working. I never gave him any grief about it. Pregnant or not pregnant, he was going to find an excuse for why he couldn't secure a job. In the three years we had been together, his total accumulation of time working added up to about three months. It was obvious that his priorities didn't involve work. I could have dealt with it better if he didn't go out of his way to be angry and bitter all the time. Jason found something daily to fight about. The once-a-day fight had become the several-times-a-day fight.

I had taken my ring off to clean it and had left it in the jar of cleaning solution. I had gone to work the next morning, forgetting to put it back on. When I got home, Jason started accusing me of doing it on purpose. He said that I did it so I could meet someone on my lunch hour without them knowing I wasn't single. I got the ring and put it on, thinking he would calm down. One thing led to another and he started hitting me. I couldn't hit him back because of the baby. All I could do was take whatever he was dishing out. He said, "If you're not gonna wear the ring, then you don't need the finger." He grabbed hold of my finger, bending it backward until it "popped." The popping ended the fight. My finger was swelling up around the ring rather quickly. I could tell that an emergency room visit was needed. Once in the emergency room, they had to cut off the ring from my finger. I found cutting the ring off a bit ironic. Jason had gotten angry about me not wearing it, and here he was, responsible for it being cut off. I had to go to an orthopedic doctor the next day to have a cast put on. They ended up casting my ring finger and pinky finger together. At least it was my left hand. The doctor told me to take a few days off work to avoid re-injury, but I went to work anyway just to keep from being at home.

May 30 came. I went to work to keep myself occupied and keep myself from getting too nervous. The day came and went without incident. I was worried. The baby was due and didn't come. Jason said everything was fine and not to worry. I couldn't help but worry—this was a long time coming, and almost wasn't. It was hard to sleep. We went to bed about eleven o'clock, and I finally fell asleep around two o'clock. Next day, it was the same thing—no baby. I was really stressing at this point. I had Jason call the doctor, who reassured me that everything was okay. We went to bed that night at ten o'clock. About eleven-thirty, Jason turned over and said his water broke. We called the doctor and headed for the hospital. They put Jason in a room for the time being as he wasn't dilated enough. This homestretch seemed to be taking forever. I was worried that something was wrong, that there would be complications. The whole gamut of stuff ran through my head. The doctor came in, checked the dilation, and felt the head of the baby.

The doctor said the baby was already coming and hurried Jason into the delivery room. Again, it seemed like forever and a day. At 1:27 a.m., the doctor came out to the waiting room. I held my breath as he started to speak. He said, "At 1:20 a.m., you became a father. Want to know what the baby is? You are the father of a little girl."

Oh my god!!! It was a girl! That's what I wanted! Wait a minute . . . Jason lied again. I stopped wondering about the why a long time ago. All I knew was that she was here. My little girl was finally here. The nurse took me back to Jason's room and they brought her in. The nurse laid her in my arms, and I started crying. I'm here to tell you, it doesn't get any better than this. The nurse said she needed a diaper put on and asked me if I wanted to do the honors. Of course I did! I opened the blanket she had on, and as I was laying the diaper under her, she peed everywhere. The nurse started laughing. "It won't be the last time she does that," the nurse snickered. I just stared at her, my baby girl, for the longest time—she looked like me. She had my eyes. She needs to have a name. Since Jason lied about the sex, I only had a boy's name picked.

The nurse came back into the room and said they needed to take her to get things checked out. I went back to Jason's room to wait. Shortly after getting to the room, an orderly came in and said I had a phone call. He wanted to patch it through to the room. No one knew we were there, so who would be calling us? I told him okay. I answered the call when it came through, and the voice on the other end said, "Is this the Myles Swain who knows Jason Cope?"

"This is him."

"Hi, I am David Wright, with the National Enquirer. We heard about your story and would like to write an article for our magazine."

What in the hell! I don't believe this!

"How did you get this number? How did you know that we were here?"

"Someone called us and told us about you and Jason, and we think our readers would really like to hear your story. We are willing to pay you . . . several thousand dollars for the story."

"Is this some kind of joke? Who are you really?"

"I can assure you it's no joke. You can call the magazine and they will verify who I am."

"We are not interested in doing any story. We want to keep this private and want to be left alone. We're not talking to anyone, so there is no story."

"Myles, we are going to run a story. We will use what we already have. We would rather you talk to us and give us the story from your point of view, but it's not necessary to run the story."

"Please don't do this! We really don't want or need this attention. Please, for the baby's sake, just leave us alone."

"This is a big story, Myles. You guys are the first couple like this. As far as we know, this situation hasn't happened before. People are going to want to read about it. Tell you what, I'll give you a few days to discuss it, and I'll call you back."

They brought Jason back in the room and I told him about the phone call. He, like me, said no way. Can they really do that? Can they print a story without our permission? I didn't know, but I would definitely be finding out. The nurse brought the baby in for a brief visit, and then I went home, with a lot on my mind, for sure.

Early the next morning, the hospital called and said Jason and the baby could come home. I thought they kept them for three or four days before releasing them. Instinct told me they were trying to avoid any publicity or drama. When I got to the hospital, the discharge nurse said that the limousine we ordered would be there shortly. Limousine? What limousine? Something sounded not quite right. We deduced that the word was getting out, and reporters were checking the area hospitals using phony stories trying to find us. The hospital let us exit through a back entrance to avoid any unnecessary drama. We arrived home and I took the baby into her new room. It was decorated with a Winnie the Pooh theme. I was always partial to the characters and loved Tigger when I was younger.

I spent the next few days getting acclimated to fatherhood, getting up every two hours (like clockwork) with the baby. I was the one who had to get up with her. Jason said, "I'm the one who carried her for nine months, my job is over. You can have the next nine months." I gotta tell ya, it royally wore me out, but I really had no problem taking care of her. I loved what I was doing—anything "father"-related was fine by me. I never complained.

Almost a week had gone by when the National Enquirer called back. This time around, they spoke with Jason. He started out saying no but, by the end of the conversation, had agreed to meet with them. I asked him why he agreed. He said that they had offered him five thousand dollars to do the story. Jason said that he would rather speak to them so they wouldn't print a trashy story full of untruths. It was clear where Jason's loyalties laid, and it wasn't with the baby. He said they were coming to interview us the next day. We argued the point back and forth several hours before I gave up, defeated. I wasn't ready to go to bed that night—too much stuff swimming around my head, so I decided to watch some television. There was a movie called Paper Dolls on, so I watched it. It was a movie about how the modeling industry takes these really young girls, paints their faces, dresses them up, and makes them look like grown-up women. Darryl Hannah was one of the teen models. Her name in the movie was Taryn Blake. When I heard her name, I knew it was what I wanted to name my little girl. It actually was a really good movie. I didn't know at the time how she spelled her name, so I spent some time after the movie spelling the name out every way there was. The spelling I came up with was Taron. I love that name. I loved that name for her. I just seemed to fit, like it was her name all along.

The next day, as we were waiting for the magazine reporter to show, I told Jason the name I had decided. Surprisingly, he agreed. He said he liked it—no fighting or arguing involved. Weird.

The reporter arrived, bringing with him a photographer. I told Jason I wasn't going to let them photograph Taron. I didn't want her being some kind of sideshow attraction. He nodded an acknowledgment, but I was concerned.

They were friendly enough and did the usual small talk to break the ice. The reporter gave Jason a contract to look at and sign. He looked it over, signed it, and gave it back to the reporter without me looking at it. Jason proceeded to give them the story they came for. When they were through talking, the reporter said they were ready to photograph us and the baby. Rather rudely I said no way. The reporter stated that the contract that Jason just signed gave them permission to take pictures of the baby. I was livid. Since "no pictures" was out of the question, I did manage to convince them to show as little of Taron as possible. They got their pictures and left. They told us that the article would be in the issue coming out July 3. Jason, I think to pacify me, said he would put the money in a bank account for Taron for college—yeah, right.

I usually sleep like a log. The phone was right beside my head on the nightstand, but I never heard it ring. I could literally sleep through a hurricane and not even know it. That all changed when Taron was born. If she so much as whimpered, I was up and out of the bed checking on her. It was like built in sonar. I could still sleep through anything else, but anything Taron-related and I was up in a second. She and I fit together like two pieces of a puzzle. She was my sun and moon and everything in between. I found myself staring at her all the time. Everything about her amazed me. I was worried that I wouldn't be able to protect her from all the bad stuff in the world.

The week of July 3 arrived. The article came out, and we held our breath, waiting for any drama to start. And the drama did start. We had multiple windows broken out. We got countless phone calls, some good, most condemning us to the gates of hell. It's funny how something happens and people you haven't heard from in ages will call you. One of the phone calls I got was from Marie—yes, the bitch from hell who gave birth to me. One would have thought she would be happy to have found me after all these years.

"Is this true? Are you living with a he/she? Myles, I didn't raise you like that—"

"Let's get one thing straight. You didn't raise me. Remember? You abandoned us when we were two so you could go and whore around with anyone that would have you. I have a mother, and it's not you! Don't even pretend to start judging me!"

With that said, I hung up the phone. It was the last time I spoke to her directly.

Other magazines were calling, wanting to jump on the bandwagon. Television shows were calling, wanting us to come on their show. Other transsexuals wanted to come meet us. How all these people found us, called us, was crazy. It was all just too crazy. We (I) turned down all the offers. I had to change our phone number in an attempt to stop the madness. Somehow, people were still finding us and calling. I finally had to get an unlisted number. For the most part, it worked. After two weeks, most of the drama had ceased.

Mark called and said he wanted to come see the baby. Of course I said yes. When I opened the door and saw him, I instantly felt all warm and fuzzy inside. He always had a way of doing that for me. He winked and came inside. Jason was in the shower, so I took him in to see the baby. She was sleeping, so we made it brief. As we were leaving her room, he walked toward me, backing me into the wall. He leaned into my face and said, "I have to be with you." It was all I could do to stand there. That particular day, he was looking mighty fine. A noise from the other room let us know that Jason was out of the shower. We went into the living room and waited. Jason came in, we visited for a while, and Mark left. I hated watching him get into his car and drive off. Watching him drive away made me hate some of the decisions I had made in my life, namely, Jason. There was only one good thing in the last three years—Taron.

Chapter 10

The End of Hell

Taron was nine months old when she took her first step. It was shortly after that when she said her first word—Papa. It was barely audible, but audible enough to know she said it. Let me back up a little bit. Several months before, Jason and I had a big fight about what Taron was going to call each of us. He wanted to be daddy. I said, "But you aren't her father, you're her mother." That was all it took. Once again, it came to blows. This time around, I matched him blow to blow. I gave it all back to him, and then some. It would be our last big fight. So to settle the argument, we came up with a compromise. Taron would call me Papa, and Jason she would call Daddy. I agreed to this knowing that I would do everything in my power to let Taron know that I was her father, and calling him Daddy was something that she just did, because she heard Ginger and Daniel call him that. So when she said Papa for the first time, I knew she understood who I was. Someone else wasn't too happy when they heard her first word. I didn't care.

Taron was almost a year old, and Jason hadn't held down a job for more than a month. I remember doing our taxes that year, and Jason had thirteen W2s. Of course it was never his fault.

Either the bosses didn't like him, or another employee blamed something on him he didn't do. I was clearly on my own in all of this—making sure the bills got paid, dropping Taron off at daycare, picking her up after work, fixing dinner, keeping the house clean, doing the yard work; you name it, I did it. Jason mostly sat around, reading books.

Intimacy was pretty much nonexistent between us, which suited me just fine. The nausea of it all had really taken a toll on me. Jason wasn't complaining, or arguing, or fighting about it like he used to. I found it odd that he wasn't. Intimacy was always the main reason he started the fights. It was clearly by chance when I found out Jason was seeing someone else.

I was in one of those dead sleeps when I was awoken by Taron crying. I was in the process of rolling out of bed when I noticed Jason wasn't in the bed sleeping. The clock was showing 1:00 a.m. I went and checked on Taron, got her situated, then returned to bed. Where was Jason? As I was getting back up to see if the car was in the driveway, I heard it pulling into the drive. I lay back down and pretended to be sleeping. Jason came in and quietly crawled back into bed without saying a word. I kept quiet about what I knew.

The next night, I lay in bed pretending to be asleep, waiting to see if there would be a repeat of the night before. About eleven-thirty, Jason slipped out of bed. I heard him getting dressed, and I heard the front door open and shut. He got in the car and drove off. As I lay there, instead of thinking "Who is he seeing?" I was thinking, "Who would have him?" It didn't bother me in the least that he was seeing someone. Hopefully, I could use the situation to get myself and Taron away from Jason. I felt like I had this one shot, this one window of opportunity to get free.

I spent the next week or so running ideas and plans through my brain, trying to find the one solid plan that would work on Jason. What I came up with was just confronting him, throwing it in his face, and telling him that I was taking Taron and moving back home with my parents. I just had to make him believe that I meant it, even though I didn't. I meant it about the leaving, just not about the moving back home part. I would wait for him to sneak back in, thinking I was asleep. As he walked into the bedroom, I would walk up behind him, hopefully taking him by surprise. I hadn't decided when I would carry all this out. I felt that I would know when the time was right, and it would be soon.

The plan would play itself out three days later.

Jason snuck out about midnight and was coming back in around 2:00 a.m. Like I had rehearsed in my head, I waited for him to walk into the bedroom and I came up behind him.

"Caught ya!"

Jason turned around and had this "Oh shit" look on his face. His face went flush, and I knew I had him.

"Don't even try to lie out of this. I've known about you sneaking out for a while now. All this time you have been accusing me of stuff I didn't do, and here you are doing it. It's over! Do you hear me? It's over! I hope they make you happy, 'cause me and Taron are out of here! You can have everything else, but I'm taking Taron and moving back home. I've secured an attorney, and they are waiting to move forward. If you try and stop me, I will go after full custody, and I will get it. Don't think I'm playing!"

Jason started crying. He said that he hadn't been happy for a long time. He said that he had started seeing this girl a few months ago, and he really liked her. I asked him who she was, and he said it was someone who I worked with (imagine that), but wouldn't tell me who. I later found out that it was a neighbor of ours and found out that this person wasn't the first woman he had cheated with while we were together. He asked me not to take Taron away. I told him I had no choice financially. He said he would talk to Morris and see if he could come up with something. I said I would hear them out, and left it at that. I told him that I was sleeping on the couch.

It all seemed too easy. Why hadn't Jason put up a fight? Did he realize that I was serious, or did he really care for this woman he was seeing? Either way, I was finally going to get a chance to see the light at the end of the long tunnel.

When I got home from work the next day, Jason said that he had spoken to Morris about the whole situation, and they came up with a plan they thought would work. Morris had agreed to give me the house at half price if I would stay here. He would put the house in mine and Taron's name, and he would buy Jason another house somewhere in the area. Jason and his new girlfriend would be moving in together. I must have been real convincing with my threat. How could I pass that up? I said yes. I really liked the house, and it was our home—mine and Taron's. I did add one other stipulation. I wanted the cats. He never did anything for them anyway.

It took Jason two weeks to find a house and another week for Morris to close the deal. I met Morris at his attorney's office to sign the papers on my house. Jason was packed up and gone a week later. I'll never forget it. Jason called the first night he was gone and said he had made a mistake. He said he was coming back. Oh hell no. I told him that he made his bed; now he could lie in it. I told him I changed the locks and he was not welcome there. He called me an asshole and hung up the phone.

It was over.

Like it was when Aunt Helen dropped us off, I spent some days worrying that he would come back, worrying that it was a dream I would wake up from. It would be two years down the road before I would really stop worrying. Two years might seem like a long time to some people, but after what I had been through, lived through, I was surprised it didn't take longer. Other than Taron, I spent those two years alone. I didn't even think about another relationship, that is, with the exception of Mark.

I went to another tattoo shop that first week and had Jason's name covered up.

Chapter 11

On the Way to Normal

I hadn't spoken to Mark in a while, not since he came to see Taron after she was born. I called him and asked him to come over. I would save the news about Jason until he got there. He showed up about an hour later. He walked in, commenting on the house looking empty—Jason had taken a good amount of the belongings we had accumulated. Without missing a beat, he turned to me, smiled, and said, "Jason moved out." I confirmed, filling him in on the details leading up to the final breakup. We spent a few hours talking about everything. Every few minutes Mark would throw "Let's go upstairs" into the conversation. I would smile, but I couldn't help but feel somewhat uncomfortable. It wasn't Mark; it was feeling like Jason would come down the stairs at any moment to tell me I was worthless. I let Mark know how I was feeling—like I was damaged goods. He moved closer to me on the couch, cupped his hand behind my neck, and told me it wasn't my fault. He said everything that Jason did to me was Jason's fault. All those things—they were Jason's decisions, not mine. It was not a reflection on me; it was a reflection on Jason. Mark sat back in the sofa and pulled me into him. We sat there, my head against his chest, his arm around me, in beautiful silence for some time. It was one of those moments. He whispered, "I won't push you to go upstairs. You'll know when it feels right." I said, "Oh we're going upstairs . . . just wanted to soak in you being here." We got up from the sofa and went upstairs. And let me say this, it was well worth the wait. Mark was a beautiful man. The details of that night I would like to keep to myself. It was one of those moments in time, playing out exactly as I had pictured it over and over again in my head. I will say that, after Mark fell asleep, I lay there watching him, listening to him breathe. This is what I had been missing. In a way, I enjoyed that more than anything else that happened. Even now it makes me smile thinking about it. That night I will always remember. It was a beginning . . . of bringing me back. It was also the last time I ever saw Mark. Not sure why exactly. Maybe it wasn't meant to be. Maybe we both had things going on in our lives, things that took us in different directions. Maybe that one night was just that—one night, which we both needed at that particular time. Whatever life had planned for me from this point on, I didn't know; I do know that Mark was, and will always be, someone very special from my life. The love of my life? Close.

I took Taron to the movies for the first time when she was four. I was worried about her calling me Papa instead of Daddy, worried she would be confused and not understand. The movie was An American Tail. In the movie, a little Russian mouse named Fievel gets separated from his family. Throughout the movie, Fievel calls his dad Papa. At some point during the movie, Taron looked at me, and I knew she understood. She knew that Papa was Daddy.

Taron was going back and forth between houses every week. One week she was with me; the next week she was with them. I hated the whole setup. I felt like Taron didn't have a home base, one place she clearly knew as home. She seemed quiet, and I didn't want her to close up inside. I tried talking to Jason about it, but he wasn't listening. On November 1987, I spoke with an attorney about getting full custody. Taron had been doing the every-other-week thing for three years now, and it needed to end. She had recently started vocalizing about not wanting to go over to the other house. She knew I was her father and didn't understand why she had to go to Jason's house. Full custody would give Taron what she needed—security, and her father full-time. Through the attorney, I managed to get a majority of the custody. I had Taron through the school year with her going to their house every other weekend. She went to their house for the summer, with me getting her every other weekend. I didn't really like the setup, but it gave her some stability. Taron hated going to their house. She would always cry when the time came around. It broke my heart when she would call me at work crying her eyes out. The last day of school was always really bad for both of us. It meant that she would be gone most of the summer. I did my best to explain why to her, but it didn't do any good. A father is supposed to fix everything and make it better for their children, but this I couldn't fix. It was all nice and neat, and legal. My only comfort was in knowing that, when Taron turned twelve years old, she could decide legally who she wanted to live with. I knew it would be me, and it couldn't get here fast enough.

Chapter 12

The Evil Twin

The next couple of years came and went without much disruption in the routine of our lives. On May 1990, out of the blue, my twin called me. I hadn't seen or spoken to Michael since 1977, when we graduated high school. He said he was in Atlanta attending a seminar and wanted to know if I was interested in getting together. I said yes, but it was a hesitant yes. My twin had this thing about him—wherever he was, trouble was close behind. At least it was like that when we were in high school. He had a problem with taking things that didn't belong to him. He faked a robbery in my parents' house, stole my dad's credit cards, stole stuff from school, forged our younger brother's name to his savings account and wiped it out, and numerous other things. It had been thirteen years; maybe time had changed him.

I drove into Atlanta that evening with Taron so she could meet my identical twin. When he opened his hotel room door, Taron said, "Papa, he looks just like you do!" We visited briefly, and I took Taron to the sitters. My brother and I hit the Midtown bars 'til the wee hours of the morning. We had a blast together. It seemed like the last thirteen years hadn't happened, like we

111

had never been apart. He flew back to Houston that afternoon. About a month later, he called again. He said that he was having problems in Houston and wanted to get away, relocate to Atlanta. I told him he could move in with me and Taron until he got situated. I had two conditions to him moving in—no drugs, and he had to get a job. He agreed. He said it would probably take him until August to get here.

In July, I had started seeing someone. His name was James. I was thirty-two, and he was forty. I kinda liked that—being with someone older. The physical attraction was definitely there. James had dark hair, icy blue eyes, moustache, and a light beard. He was very striking to look at. I found it odd that he, in all his glory, would tell me that I was handsome. I didn't hold a candle to him. Our relationship got very intense quickly. With one exception, James was almost perfect. He was very codependent. It was very exhausting to deal with sometimes. He wanted me with him every night. I would tell him that I needed to be at home on certain nights, and he would really get stressed.

His life would get put on hold until he saw me again. Some people would call that jealousy, but it wasn't anything like it. This was different. He totally trusted me, and I trusted him. He just wanted to be around me 24/7. James would call me at work just to hear my voice for a minute, and then he would hang up and be okay.

James really loved my paintings. I was currently painting in acrylics on canvas. I probably had about seventy paintings hanging in my house. It was hard for me to let them go after I painted them. They were a part of me, and selling them felt like I was selling a part of myself. James was the one who got me to the point where I could let them go. I loved him for that. After selling three or four of them, it didn't bother me anymore. I actually sold about thirty-five paintings that year. James was very good for me. It was the first positive relationship I had been in, and I liked the way that felt.

August rolled around, and my brother made the move to Georgia. He got settled in, found a job his first week, and things were good. Things were good until I got a phone call at work from a car title pawn place saying I was behind in my payment, and they were going to pick up my car. I tried to tell them that they had the wrong person, as I hadn't pawned my car. After arguing with them for several minutes, I told them I would come by on my way home. I started getting one of those bad feelings inside. The place was located in Douglasville, where I lived. I walked in the front door of the business, and they said, "Hi, Myles." I had never met these people. I asked them to see the original paperwork. When they presented it to me, it all made sense. My twin had taken my car title with my driver's license and said he was me. The date on the paperwork showed that he had done this the first week he moved in with me, almost two months ago. I called the police; they came and met me at the pawn title place. They told me I could pay the loan, have my brother arrested, or both. I told them I wanted to talk with my brother first. The officer said he would give me two days before acting on the forgery. I came home and confronted my brother. He apologized, saying he really needed the money to pay off some bills back in Houston. The apology seemed genuine. I had pretty much decided to let it go, forget about it and forgive. That phone call from the pawn place must have had some kind of snowball effect, 'cause the next day, all hell started breaking loose.

The sheriff's department was at my door the next morning looking for my brother. He had written several checks that bounced. When he got home from work, I again confronted him. He said it would all be taken care of the next day. So the next day went, and a detective came knocking. They thought they wanted to talk to me about some forged prescriptions that were being written and filled. They had been following my car for several weeks and watching the house. The detective also said that someone fitting my description was buying drugs out of my mailbox. Turns out it was my brother they wanted. On days when I was at work, my brother would use my car. On the drug issue, he was leaving money in the mailbox, and people were coming by to pick up the money and leave the drugs in the mailbox for him to retrieve. I sat down with the detective and filled him in on my brother. He left his business card, asking me to give it to my twin.

Later that same day, another sheriff's deputy came to the house. A week earlier, my brother had hit another car with my car and took off from the scene. The driver of the other car got the license plate number of my car as my brother drove off. When he got home this time, the front end of my car was smashed in. He had had another accident. I was furious as I asked him what happened. He said he had bumped into someone, and the people he hit took off. Does that make sense to anyone? Needless to say, I had had enough. I told him he would have to move out. I called the police and told them I wanted to pursue the forgery charge with my car title. The officer said they would secure a warrant. I really couldn't understand how someone could do so many bad things in such a short period of time. I would find out later that the list of things he did, and was doing, was a lot longer than anyone thought. The sheriff's office came to the house two days later with an arrest warrant, but my brother didn't answer the door. They called me at work and asked if they could enter the house. I told them yes. They found him hiding in a bedroom closet. So they took him in and booked him, and I have to say, I felt really bad that night. It was my twin brother, and even with all the bad stuff, I did love him. It was that love for him that had me do something really stupid. I went down two days later and posted a property bond to get him out. I was hoping a few days in jail would be a wake-up call for him. The wake-up call didn't happen. The drug use hadn't stopped. I called Daddy. He drove from North Carolina, we took my brother down to the jail, lifted the property bond, and had him rearrested. He somehow bonded out that night. When he came home, I told him again he had to move. Daddy said I was doing the right thing; it just didn't feel that way. My brother moved out of Douglasville and into Atlanta a week later, but not before calling the National Enquirer to try and have them do an updated story on Taron. It was his attempt at getting back at me and getting a lot of money to boot. It didn't work—they turned down the story.

I had James stay away during all the mess with my brother. It was all very frustrating, and I didn't want any of it to spill his way. I called him and let him know that my brother moved. He was relieved to hear the news. He said he wanted me to come into Atlanta as he had something to discuss with me. I drove to his apartment and we sat down. He said he wasn't happy in his job and wanted to move back to Houston for a while to make some money. He said it would be temporary, and we could commute back and forth to see each other. As I listened to him talk, my eyes started watering, and I couldn't hold it in. I was crying and asked him not to go. I told him that I loved him. He looked at me with eyes that looked like they had been waiting to hear those words from me. He said that he loved me too. By the end of the conversation, James had decided to put off leaving. He said he would keep looking for a better job in the Atlanta area.

It was a week later, on Friday, October 12, when I got the phone call. I had just walked in the door from work when the phone rang. I answered it to find it was a mutual friend of James and mine. What he said to me was, "Myles, I don't know how else to tell you this except to say it . . . last night . . . James was coming home from work . . . his car hydroplaned in the rain . . . he was killed."

I dropped to my knees, the phone still in my hand, and started crying.

"Is this a joke? This isn't funny!"

"No, Myles, it isn't a joke."

I stood back up, hung up the phone call, and started calling James' number. He didn't answer. I dialed it again. He didn't answer. I dialed, and dialed, and dialed. He didn't answer. I left him a message saying I got a call about him being in an accident and to call me as soon as he got the message. The sick feeling in my stomach was telling me James was gone. I couldn't stop crying. "Please, God, not now, don't let him be gone . . . I finally found him and you're taking him away . . . Please let him be okay . . . God, please let us have this one thing . . . He needs me."

I cried for the next four hours, up until I went to bed that night. I lay there in bed, waiting to fall asleep, crying the whole time. Just as I was falling asleep, it hit me. I had asked James to stay. I had asked him to stay, stay in Atlanta with me. If he had gone to Houston, he would still be alive. I didn't think I could feel any worse, but now I was.

I woke up the next morning not feeling any better. My eyes were really swollen and my headache was tremendous. I did something really stupid—I went to work, thinking it would occupy my mind. I got there and told my boss what had happened. She told me to leave and go home. I left but, instead of going home, went by James' apartment. A few of his friends were there. I walked into his apartment and instantly started crying again. It smelled like him. The entire apartment smelled like James. His friends wanted to start planning his memorial service, but it was something I just couldn't deal with so quickly. James' passing was the first one for me. I have never had to go through this before. No friends or family had passed away to this point in my life.

I waited until everyone else had left and walked through the empty rooms, one by one, ending in the bedroom. I sat on the bed and began talking to him. I told him I was sorry, sorry for making him stay. I told him I would always love him and think about him every day for the rest of my life. It was a promise I have kept. I took his pillow, his robe, and the answering machine tape with his voice on it. I drove home with our song playing continuously the whole way. Our song was "The Dance" by Garth Brooks. He would call me at work, and instead of talking, he would play that song from beginning to end, and then hang up. He did that a lot. It was the song I played at his memorial service. I didn't know how I was going to get through this . . .

It was difficult not to let Taron see me crying. I always wanted to be strong for her and did a pretty good job of just that, but this was all very alien to me. I explained it to her the best way I could, and I think she understood . . . understood that papas get sad sometimes, even when they don't want to be. I told her that each tear carried a piece of the sadness, and when all the tears were gone, the sadness would be gone.

The next few weeks weren't getting any better for me—I was still crying. I felt like I couldn't laugh or enjoy myself without feeling guilty for not thinking about James. I walked around being miserable, thinking it was some kind of penitence to be that way. I decided to seek professional help from a therapist. There was one thing I carried away from the session that got me through. The therapist said to set aside time each day that is just for James. It would be our time together. I could talk to him, say or do whatever I wanted during that time with him. When the time was up, I could go on with my life and not feel guilty. That might sound futile to some people, but it actually worked for me over time. There was one more thing that helped. During the time I was at my very worst in all this, James came to me. I had fallen asleep crying one night. I'm one of those people who never remember a dream, but this one I remember. I dreamed that I woke up, and James was standing there beside my bed. I sat up; I looked at him and started crying. He didn't speak, but I could understand his face as if he were. All I could say was, "I'm sorry." His face was telling me it was okay. We reached for each other at the same time and hugged. I woke up and found myself already sitting up in the bed, crying. I will go to the end of my days believing that he really came that night. He came to let me know that he was okay, that it wasn't my fault, and that he was watching over me. I woke up the next morning feeling so much better. I believe.

James' passing had brought a realization to the surface. During the many high stress periods in my life, it was always raining. What did that mean? When I was a child, as most children probably do, I truly loved the rain. I loved getting drenched, feeling it on my skin. That connection seems so distant and bittersweet now. People are always saying, "Remember when it rained?" But if you took the time to think about it, you'll find that you really can't.

The rain is different each time, and once it's gone, after a few days, that feeling is gone. One can go out into the next rain that comes, but it's not the same. It will either be warmer, or colder, softer, or heavier. It may be brief this time around, or last for days. The next rain will always be different from the previous one.

Trying to remember what it felt like is not the same as being there, in the moment. What is it about the rain that wears off our soul? I don't believe it does. I believe it's us that wear off from it.

Around this same time, shortly after James' memorial service, the National Enquirer called—it seemed my brother called them in an attempt to get paid for an update story on Taron again. I also think spite was part of his motive. They had also found Jason and wanted to talk with him. I managed to convince them there wasn't any story to write. This time around, they left us alone. This latest incident brought me to the decision that it was time to tell Taron the truth about her mother. I wanted to tell her so that she would be prepared to handle things that might happen if I wasn't around. It was better for her to know that her mother didn't leave her like she was thinking. The truth would definitely be an issue to deal with, but it was just that—the truth. I called Jason (it was rare that we spoke or even saw each other, and I liked it that way) and spoke with him about the matter. He was against it, but reluctantly agreed. I would have done it without his consent—just trying to be civil.

I contacted a well-reputed child psychologist in Atlanta and made an appointment to go in and see them. When I told them the situation, they agreed Taron needed to know the truth. They spent several visits getting to know and evaluating her. Their conclusion was that, mentally, she was very bright and could handle being told the truth. She scored high on all their tests. We set a date for all of us to be their together. I made sure that I was sitting next to Taron. Jason sat three or four chairs down. This meeting included Ginger, who had already been told the truth. Daniel wasn't present. It was decided beforehand that I would be the one to tell her. I told her that her mother didn't leave her. I told her that she has always been around her mother; she just didn't know it. I told her Jason was her mother. I said it was like being born with an extra finger or toe. A person gets surgery to fix the problem so they feel normal. I said it was kinda like that. Jason was born with a body he didn't want anymore, so he fixed it with surgery. She understood the process, but the shock was obvious. I reached out and took her hand, and she squeezed it with all her might. I told her I was here for her and would always be here for her. She was visibly shaken, so the doctor took her in the other room for some alone time with her. When they returned, we ended the session. Taron took my hand again and wouldn't let go. She looked up at me and said, "Papa, let's go home."

Taron had a few more sessions with the doctor before they closed the file on her. They said she was adjusting well with everything. Taron never came to talk to me about any of it, but I could tell that she was okay. She had the one thing in her life that was real to her, and always would be—me. I remember that we watched the movie Firestarter a lot. It was her favorite movie, and it seemed to comfort her. It was a movie about a little girl and her father. All they had in the world was each other. The little girl in the movie was about the same age as Taron. She was fragile, but also tough as nails. Taron was a lot like that. Taron was also very protective of me. She didn't let anyone get too close to me. I think she liked the idea of her and me against the world.

As time went by, what I had known ever since she was born was now happening. Taron didn't want to go to the other house anymore. She went, but she would fight it every single time. She was nine years old now and would have to wait until she was twelve to legally decide where she wanted to live. It was a no-brainer, but we would wait it out. Life at our house was otherwise routine and normal. Taron was very creative and artistic. She loved Barbie and was now taking her old clothes and cutting them up to make new outfits for her Barbie. I was amazed with some of the outfits she came up with. Her teachers at school would tell me that she was a trendsetter with the other kids. Whatever outfit Taron showed up in at school, the other kids would soon start copying. I know it had to have driven the other parents crazy.

Most nights I cooked. We rarely went out to eat. I thought it would show more love and care if I cooked, and it was a great bonding tool. Taron's favorite was pizza, but she didn't want store-bought or delivery. She always had to have my homemade pizza. She said it was better than buying or ordering pizza. Her favorite bedtime song was "Twinkle, Twinkle, Little Star." She wouldn't go to sleep until I sang it. I loved being a dad. At our house, I was dad, mom, cook, teacher, maid, I did it all. I didn't want Taron's life to lack any of the essentials, and I wanted her to have the best childhood possible, with as many good memories as possible. I was determined to give her the exact opposite of mine.

Taron turning twelve was a big turning point in her life. She could now decide who she wanted to be with. It was still a no-brainer—she picked me. She stayed away from Jason's house for about a month and then decided to go over there for a weekend. And that's what she did from that point on. She would go over there every now and then, and it was always at her choosing. Jason wasn't happy about it, but you reap what you sow, and he was finally getting a taste of that. I'm sure I was smirking on the inside, but I never spoke ill of Jason in front of Taron. I wanted her to figure things out on her own. I took notice over time that Taron didn't have any friends over to spend the night, and she didn't spend the night with any of her friends. I didn't want her to isolate herself and become insecure (if that is what it was), and I didn't want her to close herself off because she was being protective of me. I think in her mind, everything at home was perfect with just the two of us, and she didn't want to spoil it. When she was fifteen, I took her to one of those model search casting calls. I thought maybe it would bring her out of hiding. This particular model search had about twelve agencies present. The girls would have to walk down a line in front of all the agencies, holding up two photos of themselves. If an agency liked a girl, they would get a callback to see them later in the afternoon. Taron had gotten eight callbacks. The thousand or so girls that showed up was now only about ten. Taron had a blast, and it was exactly what she needed. One agency confirmed an appointment for her the following week. When we went in to see them, they signed her. We were both grinning from ear to ear. Her whole attitude and personality changed after that.

Later that summer, she entered a national model search contest in Teen magazine and in YM magazine. Out of nearly twelve thousand girls who entered each contest, Taron made the top ten finals with both magazines. What are the odds of that ever happening? When the magazines came out with the results and the finalists' pictures, Taron became little miss popular almost overnight. She was on local television being interviewed and was flown to New York for a week for the finals. She didn't win, but what a difference it made in her life. She was finally having friends spend the night, and she was spending the night at her friends' houses. She was no longer introverted, and I was proud as could be that my little girl was loving life.

The following summer, she was booked by an agency in Japan. She flew over and spent two months there. I had wanted to go but had just been promoted to manager at work and couldn't take the needed time off. It was the longest time we had been apart, and she was miserable. She hated it there and cried almost daily to come home. We were both happy when she finally made it back home. Taron was afraid that I would be mad at her for not making the most of her trip, but I wasn't angry. I just wanted to give her a chance to spread her wings a bit and give her a chance to be independent. All in all, it was a good experience for her. She didn't see it, but she came back a different person. My little girl wasn't so little anymore. She had grown up that summer and had done so without me there. I couldn't help but feel a little sad about it all, something I guess all parents have to cope with. She dabbled in modeling until her senior year in high school, and then she let it fizzle out.

It was May 2000. One of the all-time highs in a teen's life, the first big turning point—high school graduation—was a week away. We were both awoken by the phone ringing. It was five-thirty in the morning. Taron answered the phone. I had another thirty minutes before I had to get up, so I was trying to fall back asleep. I could hear Taron get out of bed and start moving around. I knew something wasn't right by the way she was moving around—there was an anxiety, a stress about her movements. I got up and went to her room. I opened her door and saw she was crying. She was moving around hurriedly looking very lost. I asked her what was wrong. She said that Ginger had just called, saying that Jason had shot himself in the head. Taron said she was on her way to the hospital to meet them. I hugged her and she was gone.

I knew this was coming. I didn't know when, but I knew it was coming. All that confusion, all that rage . . . it was coming. My first thought after Taron left was that Jason once again thought more about himself than he did his children. Taron's eighteenth birthday and graduation were both a week away, and he knew it. My second thought was that it could have been me with a bullet in my head at Jason's hand. I was relieved to have been far removed from Jason's influence.

Taron kept in touch during the remainder of the day, and I did my best to console her. I only got bits and pieces of information each time she called, but eventually had enough pieces to figure things out. For some time, Jason had been seeing this girl from his work. They evidently had a fight, and the girl was trying to end things between them. Jason had found her gun and was threatening to use it. She had managed to get it away from him somehow. This didn't deter Jason from getting his way. He made his way out to his car, and within moments, a gunshot was heard. They found Jason in his car, bleeding from his head, and called 911. Evidently, Jason's wife (yeah, you heard me right. Not sure when, but Jason and the woman he moved in with when he left me had gotten married. Jason had gone to an attorney and had his sex legally changed to a man) was aware of this other woman, as I was told that they had had several fights about her. That's all the information I had gotten from Taron. Over the years, I hadn't kept up with Jason's life. I never ran into them anywhere and didn't ask any questions. I think I actually only saw him maybe three times in sixteen years, and that was in picking

Taron up or dropping her off at his house. I really didn't care about their lives. There was the one time Jason confronted me about not "going along" with their lies. It seemed they would tell the childcare providers they used that he and his wife, Connie, were Taron's father and mother, as in birth parents. I would pick Taron up on occasion from their sitter, who would ask me who I was. I would tell them I was Taron's father. They would say, "Oh . . . her stepfather?" I would say no and tell them I was her biological father. They would always have this confused look on their faces afterward. I wasn't going to be a party to their lies, and I wasn't going to deny being Taron's dad. Let them scramble around trying to fix their mess.

Graduation came and went. Taron's birthday came and went. At Taron's request, I rode to her graduation with Ginger. I hadn't spoken to Ginger in several years. The recent tragedy gave us some common ground. On the way to graduation, we caught up, with Ginger doing a lot of the talking. I found out when Morris died, he had made Jason the executor of his estate. According to Ginger, and the copy of Morris's will she had with her, Morris had left each of his three grandchildren about thirty thousand dollars. They never got a single penny. Jason had signed off on the will saying it was satisfied. And as the executor, legally, that was all that was needed. So Jason and Connie had quite a shopping spree with the kids' money. It just gets better and better.

Jason didn't have a will, so the doctors were forced to keep him alive. Jason's wife, Connie, had contacted a lawyer to get power of attorney. While they were waiting for the power of attorney to come through, they had moved Jason to a hospice. Once she had power of attorney, they brought him home. There really wasn't anything else they could do for him. His wife kept him on medication for the pain, and waited.

Jason passed away three months after shooting himself.

After graduating, Taron enrolled at a local university and began working toward a marketing degree. I was again very proud of her during this time. She knew that I couldn't pay for school, so she held down a full-time job and two part-time jobs while going to school. She borrowed money only one time, and that was from my parents. It took her a while to pay back the $800, but she did it. It was a more-than-proud day for me the evening Taron graduated with her associate degree in marketing. The two-year degree took her four years to complete, but she stuck to it and saw it through. It was around a month later that she landed a job in her desired field. Her starting salary was not far behind what I was making, and I had been at my job twenty-three years already.

Taron had done everything pretty much by the book. She graduated high school, went to college, graduated, got engaged, got married, and had a baby, all in that order. When Taron was in grade school and junior high, other parents would look down at me. Not sure if it was me being a single parent or that they knew about Jason. I was always made to feel out of place—not welcome at the PTA meetings. Wonder what those same parents would say now, knowing how well Taron turned out. Funny thing, some of those same parents that looked down on me have kids who were pregnant in high school, kids who were regularly in trouble with the law, or kids who are drug addicts. Some of them were a combination of all three.

Taron was married on the beach in Florida on August 2006. It was absolutely beautiful. The day of the wedding, I went to her cottage to pick her up for the father and bride wedding photos. When I saw her in her wedding dress for the first time, it was the most perfect I had ever seen her. I was the biggest baby walking her down the beach to where the ceremony was held. It was about three hundred feet we had to walk, and I cried the whole way. I kept thinking about what one of my employees had told me. He said, "Myles, I hope that when I have a daughter, my relationship with her is like you and Taron. If I have half the relationship that you two have, then I will have been a success. I've never known a father and daughter as close as you two." Numerous times over the years, I've thought about my baby's wedding day. A lot of times, what you have imagined or pictured inside your mind is always better than how it plays out in real life. This time, it was exactly how I wanted it to be, how I wanted it to be for her.

The little Lugnut was born the following July. I was a nervous wreck, pacing up and down. I think the nurses were getting irritated of me asking about Taron so much. I thought that being a dad was the best thing ever, but being a grandpa or Poppy, as he calls me, is just as great. I'm at a loss for words sometimes watching him play, watching him learn, and just plain watching him. It's an incredible thing having children. It's an incredible thing having grandchildren. They have a way of validating one's life, negating all the bad stuff along the way. Just looking into his face has a way of making being alive worthwhile. When Taron was born, I told myself, "This is why I'm here." When my grandson was born, I told myself, "No, this is why I'm here."

Chapter 13

Finding My Friend

April 2008, nine months after Lugnut was born, Taron called me. She wanted me to guess who just left her house. I couldn't guess, so she told me—the National Enquirer. How they found her I'll never know, since she changed her last name when she got married. She said that David Wright had just left, wanting to do another story. A couple in Oregon was going through the same thing Jason and I had gone through. Both of them were female. Since we were the first, they wanted to do an update as part of the new story. She told him no and asked him to leave. I hung up the phone and went outside to smoke. As I was lighting up, a white car pulled up in front of my house. It was David Wright. He said the same thing to me as he did Taron. I also turned him down. He said they were doing a story anyway (sound familiar), and I pleaded with him to not use Taron's name. I told him she just wanted to live her life in peace. She deserved that. He said they wouldn't use her name. The article came out a few weeks later, and he kept his word. Her name wasn't mentioned, but mine was plastered all through it. It seemed there was more about us in the story than the actual people they were writing about. Taron found that humorous.

It was my day off, and I was doing a whole lot of nothing. I was catching up on my movie watching. The unopened DVDs were piling up on the coffee table. The phone rang and I answered it.

"Hello . . ."

"Myles?"

"This is he."

"It's John, your brother."

John? Brother? The pause of silence let him know I was confused.

"Marie is my mother. I am your younger half brother. I thought it was time for us to connect."

He went on to tell me I also had a younger half sister named Cindy. The main reason for his call was to tell me that Marie was in prison and had been there for almost three years. She had been charged and found guilty of murder (it just keeps getting better and better). Marie was the maid for an elderly lady in Texas who lived alone. On February 1989, Marie was fired by the elderly woman after being accused of stealing money from her apartment. On April 1989, the elderly woman was found bludgeoned to death in her apartment. Marie had admitted to being in the apartment on the Wednesday before the murder, but her reason for being there changed several times as to why exactly she was there. A bloodstain on a washcloth contained DNA of the elderly woman and Marie. With that and other evidence, she was convicted on July 2006 and sentenced to twenty years. It's clear to see where my twin brother got all his "bad" genes from.

John asked me if I would write to her. He said she would really appreciate it, and it would lift her spirits as she was very depressed. Well, poor, poor Marie. I told John it would be a cold day in hell. I gave him the condensed version of my early life with her and told him thanks for calling. Marie is exactly where she belongs; it just took her half a century to get there. I did find

out in the conversation that Marie was married previously before
she married Dad and had given birth to three children—two
boys and a girl. Marie denied that they were hers. She said they
belonged to her sister. Go figure. I now have five brothers and
sisters that I have never met. One lives in Tennessee, one lives in
Texas, and as far as I know, three live in France. I don't know at
this point if I will ever see any of them, whether it be by choice
or by circumstance. My sister Dany has decided to keep in touch
with John and Cindy and has been working on finding our other
three siblings in France. I don't find it important, but I hope she
is successful for her satisfaction. It's something she has decided
is needed in her life.

A while back, I decided to register with one of those classmates
websites. I wasn't sure what I was expecting, just kind of wanted
to do it. All the people in your class who have registered are listed
alphabetically. I scrolled down the list seeing names I recognized
and was putting faces and memories with each of them. He
was there, toward the end of the list. He, who had impacted my
entire life in one way or another, was Ernie. Should I send him an
e-mail? Will he respond? An entire life has gone by, will he even
care at this point that I found him? Why should I care for that
matter? He and Millard dumped me all those years ago. I sent an
e-mail to him. Some parts of the past won't allow you to let go.
Those parts I will carry with me the rest of my days. This . . . this
I can let go of. The first day went by with no answer (you know
I was sweatin'). Day 2 came and went with no reply. I was almost
ready to chalk it up and move on when it was there. I had checked
my e-mail just before bedtime, and it was there. I didn't open it
right away—I got scared. Funny thing sometimes, you hope for
something to happen, and when it does, you're scared of it. I